Blueprints for Success

eMarketing

Winning the Internet Marketing Game

Jerry Hart

with

Bette Daoust, Ph.D.

Blueprint Books ™
Blueprints for Success
Pleasanton, California

A Penmarin Book

Copyright

A Penmarin Book
Roseville, California 95661
Phone: 916-771-5869
Fax: 916-771-5879

E-mail:
General Comments: penmarin@penmarin.com
Production: connie@penmarin.com
Editorial: ginny@penmarin.com
Marketing, Ordering, Pricing: hal@penmarin.com

Published by Blueprint Books
Post Office Box 10757
Pleasanton, CA 94588 USA

orders@BlueprintBooks.com
http://BlueprintBooks.com

For bookstore and library orders:
Midpoint Trade Books
27 W. 20th Street, Suite 1102
New York, NY 10011
(212) 727-0190
www.midpointtrade.com

Unattributed quotations are by Jerry Hart
ISBN 1-883955-49-1
First printing 2006
Printed in the United States of America

Table of Contents

About the Author

Jerry Hart is the CEO of Hart Creative Marketing, Inc., an internet marketing corporation dedicated to not just building websites, but building business, specializing in expert email marketing, search engine marketing, and dynamic database driven websites. Hart Creative Marketing aims to give people tools that ignite and excite business decision makers to maximize their success in marketing.

Hart is also recognized as a dynamic speaker and prolific writer having been published in various magazines, newspapers, and internet publications. He is the author of the forthcoming book, Blueprint to E-Marketing. (Penn Marin, Summer 2005). Hart was recently a featured guest of Office Depot's "WebCafe", a series of webinars on Marketing and Business broadcast around the world via the internet.

Hart has over 20 years of experience in marketing which includes his time as a radio morning show host for Clear Channel Communications. He currently serves as chairperson for eBig.org, a sales and marketing special interest group in the East Bay.

This book, Blueprints for Success - eMarketing: Winning the Internet Marketing Game is the second book in the Blueprints for Success series. Blueprints for Success: Leadership: Management Solution that Really Work is planned for release in mid 2006. If you enjoy this book, you will certainly want to read the next one.

WARNING-DISCLAIMER

This book is designed to provide information on eMarketing, partnering with others, and forming alliances. It is sold with the understanding that the publisher and author are not engaged in rendering legal, accounting, or other professional services. If legal or other expert assistance is required, the services of a competent professional should be sought.

It is not the purpose of the book to reprint all the information that is otherwise available to eMarketers, but instead to complement, amplify and supplement other works. You are urged to read other materials on networking and put the information to personal use. See our Resource Guide for more books and information on where and how to network for success.

eMarketing does not provide you with a get-rich-quick scheme for acquiring new business. It does, however, provide some guidance as to where best to spend your time. You should make sure that you read other materials on the same subject and come up with your own personal networking plan.

Every effort has been made to make this book as accurate as possible. However, there *may be mistakes*, both typographical and in content. Therefore, this text should be used only as a general guide and not as the ultimate source of eMarketing information. Furthermore, this book contains information on eMarketing that is current only up to the printing date.

The purpose of this book is to educate and entertain. The author, Blueprint Books, and Penmarin Books shall have neither liability nor responsibility to any person or entity with respect to any loss or damage caused, or alleged to have been caused, directly or indirectly, by the information contained in this book.

If you do not wish to be bound by the above, you may return this book to the publisher for a full refund.

ACKNOWLEDGEMENTS

First, I want to thank my most important mentors, guides, and teacher, without whom this book would never have come about.
With their love and commitment to our friendship, I was able to focus on my true nature - one of immense power, courage and love.
I am thankful to have so many supportive people in my life including the one woman who has stood by me, my mother. She provided an unconditional, no judgment attitude that seem to give me permission to create, screw up, fail, overcome, succeed, and start over again.

My deepest appreciation to Steven Keifel, my coach, for helping me embrace failure, choose a calm mind, healthy body and peaceful life. With the help
Thanks to my team at Hart Creative Marketing, Inc, who are some of the most supportive people in my life.

Foreword

I have known Jerry for a few years and have always admired his enthusiasm, integrity and his ability to convey his expertise to his clients. It is through this association that I began to realize his talents were not being spread far enough. Several of his acquaintances and friends have encouraged him to write this great book on eMarketing. Jerry has more to offer than just what you read in this book. This is your starting place to get a good sense of the direction you need to take when dealing with eMarketing.

eMarketing is a vast subject without any end as it is constantly evolving. The basic principles outlined in this book will give you a giant boost for getting started and capitalizing on what you already have going.

This book takes you through all the paces that are relevant to making money from the web and increasing (and converting) the traffic you get on your site. I consider this to be a book I could use for myself or as something to be offered to those that want the knowledge to move forward.

Let's face it, if your business is not on the web, then you are not as likely to sell as many products or services as those that are. The web is no longer an option, it is a necessity. Even on the web it is who knows you and not who you know. Jerry brings this point to the forefront when he discusses relationships that you form with your customers over the web. This point is well taken as it is the relationship you have with customers that brings them back time and time again to buy.

Jerry, I want to thank you for writing this book and being a great resource for all that you meet.

This book is a must read for everyone!

Bette Daoust, Ph.D., speaker, author, consultant, and founder of the Blueprints for Success series of books and author of the best selling *Blueprints for Success – Networking: 150 Ways to Promote Yourself.*

Introduction

If you walk away from reading *Blueprints for Success—eMarketing* with only two things, I hope they are clarity and confidence: the clarity to know you can leverage the internet to build your business on a reasonable budget, and the confidence that you have all the control to create a long-term relationship online with anyone who touches your brand. Too many lost opportunities are left untold to someone like yourself, someone who is simply searching for a clear and usable road map to eMarketing success. I want to see you express your true nature any time you touch your customers on the web.

There are many ideas you can act on within this book. The key is to take the ideas that speak to you and drive forward e-ffectively, projecting your personality, your soul, and values. Take a look around—all over the world you will see many people who appear to be actively marketing online. What's missing? Most fail to spend the extra time needed to manicure a message, make it their own, and deliver the very best. We're all so busy and so good at making excuses due to hectic schedules. The result? Most marketing communications simply fall flat or attract a surge of interest and die after a short shelf life. Bottom line: make it special every time. Why settle?

This book will not try to teach you technology, but rather focuses on action steps that ignite and excite you to try many different marketing pathways. Each chapter will point you to work incrementally each day, maximizing your time spent marketing and your outbound marketing dollars without discounting the need to wrap every emarketing box with the bow that makes it look, smell, and sound the best it can possibly be.

And so, in my own prosaic words and style, with my own perception of how to incrementally win the internet marketing game, I unashamedly offer the finished product as *the* e-marketing manual that should not be speaking above you, rather with you and where you are. I've read many marketing books that leave me feeling disconnected and unable to apply steps to my own trials and marketing tribulations.

I certainly could not personalize each problem or solution to your model of business, yet I am confident you will be inspired and armed to find those most magical marketing moments that keep you striving to do more, more of what matters most behind any marketing program, and attract the people that want to genuinely have a satisfied and fulfilling relationship with you and your business.

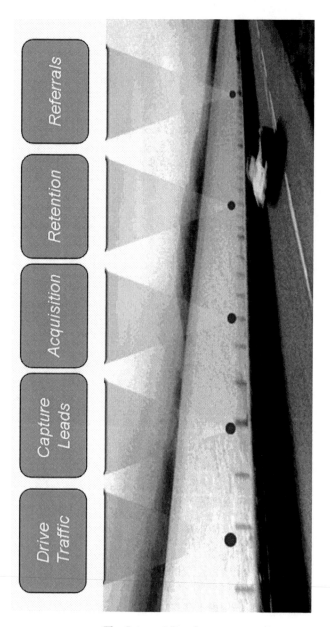

The Internet Roadmap

1. Websites, Part I

1.   The Internet Road Map

The Internet road map looks like this:

I could dive right in and propel us into a discussion of what's coming at us in the next few years—yes, the "tsunami" of business that will be coming to interactive e-mail, interactive web, interactive everything. And here's a serious warning: most marketers, let alone companies, are not really ready for the opportunity that awaits, and we'd better get our act together or else we might really blow it.

I'm talking, of course, about our industry's acne that is pop-ups, our bad hair that is sketchy content, and our halitosis that is spam. Now that I've provided a less than attractive visual let's forget about the acne, bad hair, and halitosis and move forward with action steps full of ideas on the roadway to internet success. There are five steps that drive sales and relationships offline and online.

Drive traffic: Drive traffic to the website via advertising, marketing, and communications.

Capture leads: Capture data via landing page registrations.

Acquisition: Acquire a new customer or make an acquisition defined as the desired result of a specific campaign—a sale, download, survey submission, or the like.

Retention: Duration and lifetime value of each customer.

Referral: Leveraging satisfied customers to find referrals.

The internet road map is clear in setting the route to success using the internet. However, as clear as the map may be, improving the "customer conversation" has emerged as the key missing link. The missing link is the absence of any special experience for the customer surfing on or in your website. The effectiveness can be expressed by means of moving the soul or spirit of the visitor that enters a website.

In today's highly competitive markets, it's not what you sell but how you sell that matters, and it's the same with a website. It's not what you offer on the website that matters most, it's your presentation.

Salespeople will tell me, "It's not about where I show up. It's about what I say when I get there that really counts." It's the same with a website. The customer conversation has become the last bastion of competitive differentiation. I am still baffled at how many websites look like so many others. It seems so many feel comfortable looking like everyone else on the web and have no intention to give their website the same respect as they would any other part of their brand the customer may take part in.

Today's website is a visual communicator, interactive and user friendly. Again, the communication between your website and your web visitor is communication. How you escort a visitor through your website is key to winning the internet marketing game and is done by means of careful planning and development. Certainly a website embodies promotion and education, but even more so it can embody a personality, charm, a reflection of the company's values and integrity. Consider every click of a visitor in your website and every second of their patronage an investment in you and your company.

This area of discussion is one of my most passionate topics, as I hunger to find prospects and clients who are willing to analyze what is special and different about themselves and the company they represent. This is much deeper than a mission statement or tag line, and taking what I call the "Who, What, Where, Why, and How" exercise will reveal all of the answers and provide a road map to a rebirth, a rebirth that can change a company's goals and vision forever for the better. Try it. Sit down for a moment and simply describe the "Who, What, Where, Why, and How" of your company. Oftentimes, your feelings will get in the way, and that's exactly what you want! Let the feelings flow and pull up from your heart, your soul and, of course, your experience, the most descriptive explanation of your past, present, and future.

The results from that short quiz, augmented with a marketing web design firm that has your best interest at heart, gives you a combination that no competitor could touch. Look around: most websites are not developed to be a special place. Why is the presentation of websites given less importance than brick and mortar presentation? Why do so many websites look like hood ornaments? Why are they littered with regurgitated brochure wear, when we all know we are reading less and less when surfing the web? Statistics show that not only do 80% of people visit a website never to return, they spend less than 10 seconds reading any one section of a website. Unless you're a speed reader, most pages on most websites are probably not absorbed, despite what we might think.

Starbucks is a great example of a company that found a formula it replicates through every store. The formula is special and in many ways indescribable. Try asking anyone who patronizes Starbucks to describe what they feel when they walk into their coffeehouse each day. When I ask I commonly hear, "I love their coffee." When I probe for more on what draws Starbucks fans to repeatedly spend $4.00 on coffee every day, I get very little back in response. Why? The brand is indescribable. When fans of any company's services or products are unable to define what they get back from their store of choice, you know this company has won the "branding game." Funny as it may sound, the moment a customer can define a brand he or she enjoys, the brand may have lost that special touch it once had.

In the brand is a carefully crafted formula. You have it in you, and your customers are hungry to experience it too. Don't expect them to ask you to implement the formula—they can't describe the brand let alone define the formula.

The formula has the ability to move your emotions in such a manner that you're willing to pay $4.00 for a cup of coffee. Add that up over a month and you're spending close to $100.00 to get that Starbucks caffeine jolt every morning on the way to work. Amazing? Yes! The brand of Starbucks has created a cult that has sent the message back to the company. The customers have spoken and are deep into a long-term relationship with their coffee providers.

A process, a formula, and value statement backed with commitment from Starbucks we all should ponder on and then integrate the very values we've seen Starbucks execute so beautifully directly into our websites and e-mail messages. My goal is to energize you and provide a compass that will help you incrementally understand, adjust, and inject that indescribable feeling into your brand. When you reach brand nirvana, no competitor can touch you.

2. *Beyond the Brand*

A few more steps to preparing your
website for success.

After completing the "Who, What, Where, Why, and How" exercise, there are a few more steps to preparing your website for success. Success here means a website that is leveraging your money and time while drawing your visitor closer and closer to acquisition and a long-term relationship with you. Yes, a website can be educational and built to drive sales through promotion and, above all, project the individuality of your company's unique selling proposition and differential from your competition.

The plan to accomplish this is outlined here in this quick summary of the five most important marketing tools for concisely communicating your know-how:

- A clear written statement of who your clients are (basic demographics); their values and motivations (psychographics); what problems, issues, and challenges they are facing; their aspirations and goals; and where and how these clients can be located and connected with.

- A crystal-clear marketing message that you can deliver verbally (audio logo) that tells (a) who your clients are and why they need you, (b) what actual results you can produce for them, and (c) what makes your services, approach, and results especially relevant to your clients' specific needs.

- A one- or two-page "Executive Summary" that sums up all of the above and also includes a concise success story, a brief snapshot of your services, and a call to action to find out more. This multi-purpose document can serve as a handout at networking functions, a follow-up to an in-person meeting, or even as the homepage of your website.

- A complete set of marketing materials, usually on a website. This is certainly more work than the first three, but is an absolute must if you are to effectively communicate that you know your stuff. Information should include, but not be limited to, pages on: who you work with, how you work, your services, case studies, background on you and your company, free information (articles, eZine), and how you start working with clients.

- A "Core Issue Article" that makes a solid case for the need for your services. This article is not a sales pitch but an information piece that demonstrates that you know your stuff and that you are competent to help your clients. One of the best formats is "The Ten Biggest Mistakes..." that makes your readers aware of what they may be doing wrong and what they need to do right.

I promise you that if you invest the time to develop these five marketing tools at the highest level you possibly can, the fact that you know your stuff will never be in question and everyone who steps into your website or hears you speak about what you do will be drawn to you as if to a magnet.

3.   Have a Long-Term Plan

> You need a five-year plan for your website.

You just read some highlights of web strategies to implement overnight without much planning. On the converse, websites change the way an organization communicates with its staff, customers, investors, and the general public. A change in communication is a major shift for the organization. To effectively implement such a change will take time. You need a five-year plan for your website.

Let's dispel a big myth: that the internet is changing so fast, it is impossible to plan for. That is absolute rubbish. Just how exactly has the internet changed over the last eight years? Sure, it's much bigger. But how has it changed structurally? Is the website of 1997 radically different from the website of 2005? We're still using HTML. We're still using hyperlinks. We're still using text and simple images. If anything, the web has become more homogenous. Have a look around. A great many websites now use the three-column layout. Black text on a white background dominates.

Where is all the multimedia? I saw more websites offering video in 1999 than I do today. Why? Because it didn't work. Do you really think an investment analyst is going to watch a tiny, choppy video of a CEO discussing quarterly results? They'll scan the transcript, read the press release, or ring someone up because it's much quicker. We live in a world where a manager can order more stock on his wireless device as he sits in the bathroom. But the same manager is so busy acting tactically that he has no time to plan for the long term. And then the lights go out. A tree falls on a power line in Switzerland. The lights go out in Italy. Should the citizens of the digital age buy candles with their broadband? Why is such a basic utility as electricity going out all over the world? Lack of long-term planning and investment is the reason.

All that fancy content management software, all those portals delivering jazzy personalization. Forget that they're going to give you a great website. You've got core issues that only long-term planning can address:

- Too many of your senior managers still don't understand the web. They use it only occasionally and thus lack practical experience. This often results in their caring more about what color a button is than what the content is communicating. They need winning over, and that takes time.

- Your staff is not being trained to create quality web content. Writing for the web is different from writing for print. It is hard, but not impossible, to get people to think web instead of print. It takes time and training.

- There is very little recognition for people who create quality web content. It's not written into their job profiles. They don't get part of their bonus because of it. If you want quality content, you must motivate and reward people to create it.

- Before you can give rewards, you need to measure the cost and value of your content. It will take a lot of time and effort to implement comprehensive return on investment models for content.

- You can have the best intranet in the world, but that doesn't mean that staff will flock to it. You may have a wonderful online bill-paying process. That doesn't mean your customers will automatically use it. Habits take time to change.

4.   Opt-In Forms and Landing Pages

> Optimizing your e-mail opt-in process is one of the most important tasks.

Now to one of the most overlooked areas of web marketing. The challenge: reducing the count of window shoppers that visit a web site once and never return. Reasons for abandonment are not always what might seem to be the intuitively obvious: that the product or service was irrelevant; rather, information that lacks relevance or is difficult to find is at the top of the list of why web surfing feels like web suffering.

Optimizing your e-mail opt-in process is one of the most important, though often forgotten, parts of your e-mail/web marketing program. How you present your opt-in pages and forms determines the rate of list growth and the quality of your list, and establishes subscriber expectations that subsequently drive e-mail performance. In this section, a colleague and friend of mine adds his two cents—Loren McDonald, VP of Marketing for EmailLabs, presented the following four valuable points that speak to high-impact, high-conversion-rate opt-in pages:

1. Getting People to the Opt-In Page
Once someone is on your website, how do you get them to the opt-in page?

- **Don't hide the link:** If your e-mail newsletter/promotion is key to your business, make sure that it is easy and obvious for website visitors to find the signup page. Consider including links in main and secondary navigation and promotional boxes in sidebar areas. Don't make your visitors search to see if you offer an e-mail newsletter. Include some form of link on every page of your site.

- **Don't Disguise It:** When referring to your e-mail in links and navigation areas, don't use some name or term that isn't obvious to all. For a link, "Newsletter," "E-newsletter," or "E-mail Newsletter" is fine.

- **Home Page:** If appropriate, promote articles and news from the current issue on your home page and then link to article/issue.

- **Back Issues/Articles:** For newsletter publishers, make sure you have an area of your website such as a "Knowledge or Resource Center" where you keep archived issues and individual articles pulled from the newsletter. Then promote subscriptions to your newsletter throughout this area.

- **Web Version Subscribe Link:** If you post your back issues on your website, make sure they include a "Subscribe" link within the actual e-mail.

- **Product Pages:** For online retailers, consider including copy in a prominent spot such as: *Signup for Retailer X's free bi-monthly newsletter and get special deals and sales only available to newsletter subscribers.*

2. Copy and Design/Layout of Opt-In Page

There is only one purpose of your e-mail opt-in page: to convert as many visitors as possible to subscribers. Its design, layout, and copy, therefore, should be similar to that of a landing page. A landing page is simply the page an e-mail recipient is directed to from any number of media.

- **Clean and simple:** The opt-in page should be designed in such a way that the images, copy, and form instill confidence, trust, and value.

- **Samples:** Always include a link to a sample copy or copies of your e-mail and consider including a hyperlinked small screenshot of your e-mail.

- **Testimonials/awards:** Use testimonials in pull-quote format, either text or as an image, that highlight awards or kudos that readers and third parties have bestowed on your e-mail publication.

- **Incentives:** Offering up an incentive or discount is a great way to increase conversion. Whether it is a "free white paper" or "$5 off your next purchase," incentives work.

- **Value proposition:** Subscribers are happy to provide you their valuable e-mail address, but only in exchange for something of value. It is important that your opt-in page copy and images convey the core value of your e-mails. For example, if you are a retailer you should highlight things such as "e-mail only specials," advance notices of sales, and other values they will receive as an e-mail subscriber. Newsletter publishers should stress things such as the type of content, timeliness, your expertise, and the content relevance to readers.

- **Privacy/e-mail policy:** We recommend that you include a brief one- or two-sentence e-mail policy located near the form "submit" button and a link to your company's more detailed privacy/e-mail policy. For example: *Hart Creative Marketing, Inc., will not use your e-mail address or information for any purpose other than distributing the Hart Creative Marketing, Inc., E-newsletter and related special materials.* Then supply the user with a link to the complete privacy policy available for viewing online.

- **Expectations:** Lastly, the copy and layout should set expectations for the recipient. This includes the frequency of the e-mails and whether they should expect other communications from your organization—and, again, accurately convey the value of the e-mail. Further, clearly explain your confirmation process if you are using a double

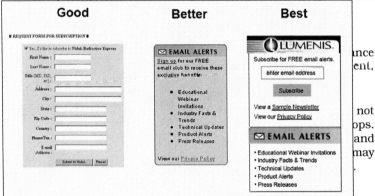

- **Don't ask for too *little* information:** By the same token, plan for the future. The most often missed opportunity on the Internet Road Map is the acquisition. Focus on acquisition of an e-mail address when a visitor arrives on your website. Remember the two key points on the internet road map are driving traffic to your site and, once they arrive, capturing their e-mail address.

- **If you accomplish only one thing** from that one visitor on your site, acquire their e-mail address to begin an ongoing relationship filled with respect, frequency, and more sales.

Above you can see three forms. Ideally, the best example is only requesting an e-mail address.

Now you have two different approaches with terrific results you can try for yourself.

Option 1

When the visitor enters the e-mail address and clicks subscribe for the free e-mail alert, he or she is directed to a page that displays that same e-mail address and invites the visitor to enter more information about him- or herself; the visitor may even answer any questions you have posed. I would only ask questions to the new subscriber if I had a wonderful gift of some kind, such as a free report or a grand prize giveaway.

Option 2

On the home page the user enters the e-mail address and is then directed to a landing page where the user is thanked for subscribing and told to expect a follow-up e-mail that will contain a link to a special section of your website where your new subscribers can update their contact information. We call this a preference or profile center. Preference and profile centers are discussed further in Chapter Four and are just as important to have on your website as the e-mail data capture box you see above. Adding the privacy policy link and a note promising "to never share the visitor's e-mail information with anyone" is highly recommended.

While only asking for someone's e-mail address makes the signup process extremely quick, you have not obtained information that will help you deliver more relevant e-mails to your subscribers. This includes format preference, name, and other preferences/demographics key to your program.

Address validation: To ensure that subscribers enter their e-mail address correctly, include a script that checks for syntax errors upon submission. Additionally, consider a secondary box that requires them to re-enter their address. This will minimize invalid addresses due to input errors.

Form fields—the minimum:
- First name
- Last name
- E-mail address
- Format preference (HTML or Text). In addition to providing options of whether to receive HTML or Text, consider including a note such as the following: *(Text is recommended if you use Eudora Light, Eudora Pro 3 and below, Lotus Notes versions below R5, or AOL 5.0 and under.)*

Form fields—optional:

- Secondary e-mail address. Since approximately a third of those on your list will change their e-mail address every year, consider asking for a secondary e-mail address. Then when their primary address bounces you can send a follow-up e-mail to the secondary address.

- Frequency. Many sophisticated retailers and publishers give subscribers the choice of how often they wish to receive e-mails, i.e., daily, weekly, monthly.

- Demographics such as gender, age, location, etc.
- Interests/preferences such as topic, rock vs. jazz, etc.

3. Other Opt-In Pages
In addition to your actual e-mail opt-in form pages, there are other means on your website of gaining new subscribers, including:

- **Download/registration pages**: Always include an e-mail subscription check box as part of your registration (download white papers, membership, demo request, etc.) forms. This approach can generate a subscription conversion rate of 50% or more.

- **Purchase/shopping cart pages:** Be sure to include product/shopping preferences in your shopping cart form and a clear opt-in check box for your e-mail.

Thanks, Loren, for all those suggestions.

5.   *Five Tips to Improve Conversion*

> **Conversion on the Landing Page is the key.**

Pointed question: "Hey, how'd that e-mail ad do last week?" Typical answer: "Well, we got a good number of click-throughs." Yep, your ad copy succeeded. But whatever you wanted people to ultimately do . . .

- Register for a webinar
- Buy or demo a product
- Subscribe to a newsletter
- Give you their contact information for some other purpose (in exchange for a white paper, an industry report, etc.)

Well, not many of them did it. Your landing page dropped the ball. But next time it won't if you follow these five guidelines:

1. Pick the one-trick pony
Your landing page should have one purpose: Persuade your prospect to take your ad's call to action. That's it. And that's why I strongly suggest creating a unique landing page for every e-mail ad, whether it's an ad you're placing in an e-newsletter or a standalone e-mail you're sending to a list. Does that mean a generic page you already have can't do double duty? No. For example, say you've bought a Google pay-per-click (PPC) ad. Someone who finds you via a search engine is specifically looking for the type of product or service you provide . . . and you may decide your homepage is the most appropriate page for the ad to direct to.

2. Focus, focus, focus
I once came across an e-newsletter ad from a large, universally known enterprise software company. The ad offered a free "kit" comprised of two white papers and a product demo. So a prospect clicking through to the landing page would be looking to learn more about the kit and how to get it, right? But the first half of the landing page copy talked exclusively about the product.

When crafting your landing page, know the path you want your prospect to take and guide him or her along it. Cut out copy that might read beautifully but actually distracts from the task at hand. And only talk about your products and services if it will enhance the value of your specific offer. In the example above, the company's product pitch could have done just that had it been (briefly) incorporated into the description of the kit.

Keep reminding yourself: "One-trick pony." The next question: How much copy does a landing page need? It depends on the ad it's following up. In an e-newsletter ad, you don't have room to say much about your offer, so your landing page must expand on it. But if it's standalone e-mail, you're able to say a lot more. So your landing page just has to close the proverbial sale. And it depends on your offer.

3. Eliminate any opportunity for hesitation
Make someone hesitate and he or she may back out, no matter how valuable your offer. So spell out as clearly as possible what steps your prospects need to take and why, and tell them how you'll use the information they give you. And in cases where your registration process extends beyond your initial landing page (which means it's not obvious to the prospect how many hoops he or she needs to jump through), state how long the process will take. Finally, whatever you're trying to get your prospects to do, make sure they can do it. One technical snag and your already time-strapped prospect may give up. So before you go live, go through the process yourself to confirm everything works. And have a few colleagues outside your company do the same.

4. Carefully formulate your registration form
What information do you want people to give you? Just name, company name, job function, and contact information? Or additional qualifying questions on top of that? And how many questions can you safely ask? If you demand too much time and effort from your prospects, you risk scaring them away. And for that reason, you might not be well served choosing a free trial or other offer that requires too much qualification. But it all depends on your objective and target audience. If the offer's valuable enough to them, then they'll fill out a longer registration form. They may even expect it. In some cases, perhaps you want to screen out anyone who isn't willing to go through the requisite hurdles! Bottom line? Prioritize. Figure out what you most want people to tell you. What's "absolutely non-negotiable" if someone wants your offer? Then ask for it. Have other questions you want to ask? Consider leaving them out.

5. Test!
You've seen the phrase "it depends" above more than once. Which predictably leads to this assertion: There's no such thing as a perfect landing page. So experiment! If possible, see if you can test two landing pages via an "A/B split." This means that half the people who see your ad will arrive on one landing page if they click the link and the other half will arrive on the other one. You can test the phrasing of qualifying questions. Should you have longer copy or shorter copy? Should you ask fewer questions or more questions? See what works best and apply what you've learned to future campaigns. And make sure to test only one variable; otherwise you won't know what's causing the difference in conversion!

Pick up more tips on improving your landing pages in Chapter Six.

6.   Increase Website Conversion Rates

**A few more steps to preparing your
website for success.**

In a recent meeting, I was asked several specific questions about how to improve website conversion rates— converting clicks to customers. Here are my answers.

What do you mean by conversion? Do you mean getting someone to answer the simplest call to action such as "read more here," or actually selling a product or service?

What you're talking about here are two different ways to measure your website. "Read more here" is what I would call a variable affecting your conversion rate. I call these kinds of variables "micro conversions" because they are all small (microscopic, even) steps toward full conversion. A micro conversion is something that you should test and measure. "Read more here" might not get as high a click-through rate as "Click here to find out how to win a month's supply of vintage wine." So by improving this click-through, you get the person browsing to take another small step toward your final website goal. By doing this, you improve your overall conversion rate, which in this case is to get someone to register or subscribe to win a month's supply of vintage wine. Micro conversions can be tracked by measuring the click-through of links, or the read time for content, or the bounce rate for headlines and copy. Full conversion means persuading your visitors to do what you want them to do. In my example, it would be registering to win wine. But it could be subscribing to a newsletter, downloading an audio file, buying a product, selling a service, or whatever. It should reflect your website's business objective.

What strategies would you suggest when no online conversion is possible? I need them to call me for more info, to learn more and to eventually give them a proposal.

There is no such thing as "no online conversion." You're looking for leads that will eventually phone you, but the visitor is the one with the power. If you don't give your visitors a reason to let you continue to have a dialog with them, then they won't. Using opt-in is one answer. If, for instance, you ask for a name, e-mail address, and telephone number from your visitor so that she or he can then get useful information from you in the form of a free report or audio file, you do two things. First, you qualify the visitor as someone who is interested in your services, and second, you get permission to contact him or her again.

Rather than expecting someone to pick up the phone, you need to build into your website a powerful reason for your visitors to give you permission to e-mail or talk to them. In your case, you say they need to ring you to learn more. Put what they need to learn into some form that they can opt-in to get, such as a white paper, report, or audio file. Then you have a conversion rate that is the percentage of people who give you permission to continue the dialog with them by giving you their e-mail address or phone number so that they can learn more about your offering. People visit a website to get information, so give them the means to get it.

What if the product that you sell is also sold by several others on other websites? How do you get someone who is browsing the internet to notice your site and want to order from you?

In offline marketing, a successful tactic is differentiation. It's no different online. If you stand out from your competition, you get noticed. What makes you different (not necessarily better, just different) from your competition? A USP (unique selling proposition) makes an enormous difference to conversion rates. For example, we improved subscriptions by 11% per month for six months by differentiating ourselves.

The second point is that your site should be of use to your visitor. The one thing that all people online have in common is that when they browse they are looking for information. So give your visitors what they want in the form of education. If your potential customers become educated about your offer and take away something useful from your site, they will remember you over your competition.

How do you get the address, telephone number, and name of the owner of any company that you're trying to get in touch with to see whether they might be interested in what you sell?

You need to get permission from the visitor to get that information. It can't be done with any available tracking tools. There is a very good reason for this, and it's called privacy. If you or I went online and could have our names, addresses, and phone numbers tracked by software, it could be potentially dangerous.

Imagine if you were online talking in a chat room about going on a vacation in a faraway land for the next few weeks, and your personal information could be gathered. The person who sees that information then knows when to go to your address and rob you while you're away. It's all right to track browser behavior, because no personal details are ever tracked.

What should one look for in the web logs to determine conversion rates?

Web log files are a problem because they record everything. Web logs record every request to your site's pages from search engine indexes, e-mail harvester software, link harvesters, and visitors.

So first, you need to filter out from log files the information that isn't relevant to visitors. Then you're looking for unique visitors (not visits) or unique sites. Once you have that filtered figure, you have the approximate number of visitors coming to your site. It's still not 100% accurate, because proxy servers record multiple visitors as one browser, but it's as close as you can get with log files.

Then, divide the number of people who complete the conversion action by the total visitors. That is your conversion rate. If you can get software that doesn't use logs, such as IRIS Metrics, or log software that works out the filtering, such as Web Trends, your job is much easier.

What factors have the biggest impact on conversions on my website?

The short answer is differentiation, target marketing, your site's relevance to your desired audience, measurement, experimentation, and (most important) trust. Differentiation is the first step in the process. You must find a way to stand out from the competition. It should start with the domain name and continue throughout your entire website's strategy. Then, in your content, your copy and your design, you must smack your target audience between the eyes. You have to find out exactly what it is they want and answer the wants and needs of that audience.

Relevance is hugely important, too. If you're running a campaign on Overture or Google with certain keywords, your audience should land at exactly the right place after typing those keywords and finding your website. So, if members of your audience type "Red Vintage Wine" into Overture and your link appears, on clicking through they should be taken to your page that talks all about, and sells, red vintage wine. Those visitors shouldn't land at the home page of your website, which probably has a small link to the red vintage wine section and five or six other types of wine for sale.

Then, measuring and experimenting are key to improving conversion rates. You can't improve conversion without measurement unless you're making educated guesses (or you're just plain lucky). So, get a good measurement system, learn what it's all about, and test your changes.

Finally, and most importantly, there's trust. You can't sell anything if your audience doesn't trust you. You can start earning that trust by prominently displaying your privacy policy and your shipping procedure. Also, clearly state that you use SSL encrypted protection for the forms on your site and that hundreds of satisfied customers have already bought from your store. And make it very easy to find your contact information, such as a name and address, in addition to providing support via e-mail. For the longer term, you could educate your audience via your website with articles and "how-to" sections or newsletters. Doing so will instill trust over time. In short, your prospect must trust you to part with his or her money.

7. *More Website Conversion Strategies*

> **How do you go about consistently improving conversions?**

Now, let's look at measurement software tools, the pros and cons of logs versus ASP vendors, average conversion rates, and why it helps to track visitor activity using available software. We'll also talk more about what you should test and tweak to improve conversion rates. Does it help to track website visitor behavior with software? "Yes" is the simple answer. Here's why: If you don't measure, how can you know what to improve? With effective tracking software, you have facts in front of you. Effective measurement, though, is more than simply having good software; it's analyzing why things happen. One thing that we measure is bounce, the number of people who arrive at a specific page and then leave without doing anything. The lower the bounce rate, the better (obviously). A low bounce rate means that people are using the site effectively.

A recent client is a perfect example. She had two pages with different articles on her site, with exactly the same navigation left and center. Most articles had a bounce rate of about 53%. But one had a better bounce of about 50%, and another had a much worse bounce of around 90%. We analyzed both and found that the one with the 50% bounce was much more relevant to the reader arriving at the page. Specifically, it had better and more relevant links at the bottom of the article. We concluded that being relevant on the poorly performing page in the same way would reduce the bounce rate. We would simply not have known that this problem was occurring at all without tracking software.

What measurement software tools would you recommend?

I use IRIS Metrics. I would also recommend browser-based software such as Websidestory, HitBox, WebTrends Live, RedSheriff, and Omniture. Generally, you get what you pay for. And while these systems are not cheap, they do provide the level of detail required to run an effective web campaign. People have asked me if it's possible to use Webalizer, which is free log software, to run an effective web measurement campaign. While it's possible to get a lot of useful information from free and cheap systems, you don't get truly useful information such as path tracking, bounce rates, repeat visitor information, accurate visitor counts, accurate page counts, and loads more information. Such information is critical if you want to base business decisions on your measurements.

What is the difference between log-based and browser-based measurement?

Tracking tools that rely on server-based measurement are typically programs that are installed on your web server (by your ISP [internet service provider], if your site is hosted) or installed locally on your PC using the log files taken from the server. Server-based measurement programs measure activity based on the text files held on the web server, referred to as log files. The way that browser-based measurement works is that information from each browser that visits your site is recorded, usually in a database, and then the data is manipulated into reports you can read. Typically, these services ask you to paste some JavaScript code into your web pages. A cookie is used to determine which user is accessing the site. This is then tracked on a remote server and you log in to view the reports. I recommend the use of ASP measurement, because it only measures how people using a web browser use your website. The log files record everything visiting your pages. They need a number of added filters to stop e-mail harvesters, search engines, and a variety of other software generated crawlers or bots from being counted as "visitors." Without the filters, you can get seriously skewed results.

Server access is often required to get log file filtering right. Otherwise, you're relying on your ISP to report your tracking correctly. The log files for one of our clients had 10 times more page counts and visits recorded than shown by using an ASP. That's an error.

What is an average conversion rate?

This is a topic of serious debate. In other marketing industries, there's no guesswork. They have standards that everyone follows. We need those same standards in the online space before any real answer can be given. Analytics companies, the big research companies, and digital media associations are going to have to come together to define these standards. Currently, we're in the process of trying to establish a worldwide benchmark with a number of other prominent people in the industry who also want to know the answer to this question. But meanwhile, here are some statistics we've gathered from different sources. I have figures for three types of websites: sales (e-commerce), lead generation, and subscription-based sites. Generally, sales sites seem to range between 0.5 and 8.0%, with the average rate at 2.3%, according to FireClick statistics published this year and figures published in 2003 by e-consultancy.com. In 2000, the average figure for sales conversion, as published by shop.org, was 1.8%. The high-end figures, I hasten to add, are the top internet retailers, according to all sources. My own experience shows that sites hit between 0.5 and 5.3%, so this seems to correlate with the published figures. Of course, since there is no defined standard, these numbers have to be taken as a rule of thumb.

The only source I have for lead generation sites is e-consultancy.com. It quotes 2 to 3% as the rate for users that complete an optional or free registration process, with 5% being best in class. Our own experience again falls in the same ballpark.

Subscriptions-to-sale conversion is typically between 1 and 7%. Again, the source is e-consultancy.com. We don't have figures for visitor-to-subscription conversion, but our experience with clients has been between 1 and 8%.

How do you go about consistently improving conversion?

It boils down to treating web marketing as a science. We do it by consistently measuring how people use a website. Over time, you will learn what works and what doesn't, and you'll stop wasting your time on the things that don't work. First, we look at the technical aspect of the site. It's amazing how many people overlook and ignore thousands of people who don't use Windows XP with Internet Explorer at a screen resolution of 1024x768. So, first, make sure that you develop something that works for everyone. Next we look at where the traffic comes from. It allows you to concentrate your efforts on your best chance of generating traffic that converts. Then we try to reduce the average website bounce rate. The lower the average bounce, the higher the number of people surfing your website and seeing the value of your offer. The higher the number who see your offer, the better the chance of a sale. Checking bounce rates also usually brings up some juicy problems to be solved. Then look at testing and improving copy and graphical content, running split tests and measuring bounce rates on copy or simply testing the click-through on links. I do much more, but the basic premise is this: test and measure; follow up with experimentation, then with more testing, and more measuring.

8.   The Kick is in the Keywords

What is the traffic potential of your keywords?

You may not be asking me for this topic, but I suggest you get to know more about how an effective keyword strategy can improve website conversion rates. My take on it is based on the web analytics evidence of our own keyword strategy.

Have you ever been in a room where people are talking, but you don't understand a thing about the topic, or perhaps even the language? It's similar online. You have to start communicating on your website using the terminology that your visitors use. If you use the right terminology and phrases, not only do they find you, but (to use my analogy) you also let them in on the joke. If you're using the wrong terminology, then you're leaving your visitor a bit confused, a bit foggy, feeling a bit left out of it all. How do you avoid this on your website? When selecting your keywords, follow three simple guidelines:

Gauge the traffic potential of the keywords in terms of quantity

Gauge the visitor's intent when using those phrases in their search query

Measure traffic potential from those keywords in terms of conversion

1. The traffic potential of your keywords

Obviously, you want the search engines to drive lots of traffic to your website. However, quantity should never be your first objective. Quality traffic should be what you're looking for. Your goal is to optimize your pages for the keywords that bring the highest numbers of prospects. Find the keyword phrases related to your industry that your target market is searching for. So, first, find out the terms that are being used by the general public by using a tool like the Overture keyword suggestion tool. Others are available, such as the one at Google. Wordtracker is also worth the investment. But before you rush off and start optimizing your site for the keywords you find, take heed of the second guideline: gauging visitor intent.

2. The visitor's intent

Test the phrase in the search engines you're going to optimize for. For instance, our own keyword research showed that "conversion website" is a phrase people are using in the search engines; however, if you search on Google using this exact phrase, you will see that people are actually looking for money conversion, religious conversion, weights, and metric conversion, etc., not sites about converting site visitors to buyers. This is why you need to look for the real reason why people are searching. In our case, "conversion website" might be worth testing on pay-per-click, but it's not worth optimizing our organic pages for that phrase.

3. Traffic potential in terms of conversion

The next step is keyword measurement and experimentation. We decided to optimize for "improving website conversion" because this phrase showed that there should be reasonable traffic levels, good intent, and a high number of conversions. We found that 27.8% of people using that search term end up subscribing to our newsletter. When people enter those keywords into a search engine, we're speaking their language, because our entire website is a resource about what they're looking for. To do this yourself, identify keyword phrases that you think fit well with the first two guidelines above, and then measure the result. It's about selecting the keywords immediately relevant to what your audience is looking for.

Checklists

Define Your Expertise

What are you currently selling on your website?

_____

_____

_____

_____

_____

What is your brand and what is your value to your customers?

_____

_____

_____

_____

_____

List 5 common problems you solve?

_____

_____

_____

_____

_____

Define Your Best Customer.

List 5 types of customers you serve.

_____

_____

_____

_____

_____

What is your value proposition? How do your customers view your value?

_____

_____

_____

_____

_____

What industries do I currently sell to?

_____

_____

_____

_____

_____

What industries would I prefer to sell to?

_____

_____

_____

_____

Creating Your Plan

List a few core messages you would like to address with your webite.

_____

_____

_____

_____

_____

Do you have opt-in forms or landing pages? Where are they located?

_____

_____

_____

_____

_____

Name at least 5 items you could use an incentive for customers to buy from you.

_____

_____

_____

If you have a newsletter, which page has the link to sign-up?

_____

_____

_____

_____

_____

_____

Customer Information Collection Checklist

Information	Reason

2.   Websites, Part II

1.   *Web Writing Dysfunctions*

What's the single most important thing that could improve the web?

What's the single most important thing that could improve the web? It's not broadband. It's better writing. The general quality of writing on the web is poor. The way you write has a major impact on what people think of you. Avoid these common mistakes and you will achieve more with your website.

Deadly Sin Number 1: I think I'm God
You cannot sell the organization by selling the organization. Face the facts. People are mean on the web. They're only out for themselves. *"We're celebrating our 50th anniversary!"* "So?" *"50% off because it's our 50th anniversary!"* "Happy anniversary!" Never, ever, start a heading or a sentence with your company name. Always start with the need of your target reader. Before you write, repeat to yourself: *"It's not about me. It's about my reader, my customer."*

Deadly Sin Number 2: I go on and on and on . . .
It is an unfortunate fact that those who have the least to say often write the most. Quality web writing is rarely about volume, and it is never about padding. If you expect someone to read more than 500 words on a single topic, it better be extraordinarily good. Get to the point. Then stop.

Deadly Sin Number 3: I can't spell and have awful grammar
If you can't spell and you've awful grammar, you're not going to make it as a business writer. Take up avant-garde fiction. But forget about writing for the web. Good web writing is difficult. It requires a lot of skill and experience. Also, sloppy e-mails create a very bad impression.

Deadly Sin Number 4: I'm locked in a print view of the world
Writing for the web is not the same as writing for print. If you can't see the difference, you need to look harder. Web writers write for how people search. They always finish their content with a set of links. They write great metadata for every piece of content they write. Web writers never say: "How do I quickly get this brochure up on the website?" I know poor content is worse than no content. Amateur content makes you look like an amateur organization. Nobody should be managing a website unless he or she has a deep understanding of content.

Deadly Sin Number 5: Don't have five points if there're only four

2. *Putting Personality into Your Website*

Deliver and present that content to readers in a professional manner.

People visit your website for the content. So, ideally, you're giving them content that's timely, relevant, and useful (and sometimes even entertaining). Deliver and present that content to readers in a professional manner and you have yourself a winning newsletter. Well, almost. Most of you have competitors. There's no reason why they can't publish valuable content, too. In fact, it takes considerable skill, innovation, and effort to stand out through content alone (just ask those who've managed it). Injecting personality into your publication is one way to give yourself a little edge in the battle for the hearts and minds of the market. You're probably using your newsletter to "build long-term relationships and a better rapport with customers or prospects." Valuable content is the foundation on which this is based. Personality is the icing on the content cake. A little dose of personality helps build that reader rapport and adds uniqueness to your publication; it's something competitors can't copy so easily.

The right personality can also complement the image of your brand, products, services, or company, essentially reinforcing whatever impression or message you're trying to communicate. Which is all well and good, but what is this personality? No doubt there are various dictionary definitions, but I prefer to think of it like this: If content is what you say, then personality is how you say it. It's the sum of all the distinctive characteristics that make your website's voice and writing unique: your style, tone, humor, emotion, vocabulary, attitude, and more.

So how do you give your website the right dose of the right personality? Think of your website as a one-on-one conversation. Just imagine sitting in a coffee shop talking informally with a customer. That's the starting point for your approach—a more personable and appropriate "human" voice will come naturally. When you picture the coffee shop scenario, you quickly see how inappropriate (not to say ridiculous) some of the more traditional styles of customer communication can sound on a website. Drop the jargon, drop the sales pitch, be as honest as you can, and talk like a human being. Refreshing idea, isn't it?

The personality of the writing itself needs to gel with the other elements of the website, particularly your image, content, audience, design, and objectives. What's appropriate and what isn't? Only you can answer that question. Ideally, have people write the content that fits the required personality naturally, who can write as themselves, subject to a few publication-related constraints. If you need to define specific personality "rules" that people should follow when writing or preparing content, then ensure they're closely defined and easily understood. Then appoint someone to act as guardian, someone who can read the content and spot inconsistencies or aberrations in the personality projected. This kind of defined personality can sometimes better fit your needs, and ensures consistency, even when the writing or production team changes. It also lets you build a personality around some other element of your business (an advertising spokesperson, your product, your CEO, whatever. . .).

You can have as much or as little personality as is appropriate. But what if people don't like it? You can be pretty sure some people won't like your tone or style. And that's a good thing, too. It's hard to get anyone engaged in your website if you're trying to be all things to all people. Most importantly, the potential loss of a few subscribers is well worth the additional rapport you'll have with those who remain. Or you can be very boring, very dry and very safe, and disappear in the morass of your competitors' offerings.

I've also come across websites where tooting your own horn turns into the "let's talk about me website, and by the way have I told you, it's all about me on this website."
You need to find the right balance; small doses of "personal" information tend to work well in terms of relationship building. But be very careful not to overdo it. Be especially careful with the use of opinion. On-topic opinion is a good thing and can be a great content element. But while talking about your dog can, at worst, provoke uninterest, sounding off on unrelated topics can actively offend. Take care, and don't let a newsletter become anyone's ego vehicle.

I also enjoy a picture of someone looking friendly and attractive on the website. A human voice can even be better through audio. It is easier to connect with people at a more human level if they can relate to a name or face, whether invented or real. So sign editorials, give authors a byline, or list some names down in the administrative section of each issue.

Take a look at your favorite websites. Sure they'll have great content, but what else is it that makes them stand out in your inbox? I bet you it's the voice and personality that do it.

3.   *Discussion Boards and Chat Rooms*

Pointing other users to your website is a great technique to generate leads.

Some discussion boards are patrolled for quality control, and those are clearly not helping the brand of the company where you might collide with a chump who feels he can spray his verbal graffiti all over a thread or forum within a discussion board. Even so, going to a discussion board within your vertical and pointing other users to your website is a great technique to generate leads and build your e-mail house list. A house list is your opt-in permission-based e-mail list. Most discussion boards will allow you to post your web address, especially if you present a value to the audience reading the website. Here's a great opportunity to push traffic to your opt-in page, where you have a clear e-mail capture window and an offer to acquire that new e-mail address.

This is a terrific direction to travel when your intent is to drive traffic back to your site, where you capture an e-mail address, start your relationship with this new visitor to your website, and keep in touch with multiple e-mails until your opt-in e-mail recipient soon converts to a valuable sale. Remember, a conversion may also mean signing up a for a free teleseminar.

Conversion may not always mean loading up the shopping cart and checking out for a final sale. Discussion boards support my theory that people use the net to get educated as well as to buy. When you drive people into your site using an educational platform like a discussion board, you're bound to push people who want more information on what you're talking about into your site to ignite your new visitor into a new lead worth dripping on for a sale down the road.

Remember, education plus promotion equals a win on the internet road map.

Installing a discussion board on your website is logical if you have someone to keep the discussions fresh. Old content is tired, disappointing, and irritating, especially when I expect to be fed with new material and instead I stumble into stale content. The sites around the world that have successful discussion boards are sites that understand a mandatory connection to the home page. Here's what I mean.

Add a placeholder on your home page that highlights a headline from the discussion board. The headline might be endearing or even controversial. The point is to drive traffic from the home page into a discussion board. The real winners of this strategy are those websites that will encourage a user to log in if he or she chooses to post any feedback in the discussion board. This is called a dynamic website, that will request that a user log in with name and password prior to having permission to post individual feedback on the site. This ensures you know who is posting information on your site and who is or isn't following proper online etiquette.

Most well greased discussion boards run around $100 for the year and can be branded to fit your company's brand for as little as a few hundred dollars. Make sure you uphold the brand of your company and match the flavor of your discussion board with the style you have integrated into your site design.

Chat Rooms

Chat rooms are great if you have someone on staff to keep the content fresh. I don't care if you're Toys R Us, even the kids may get complacent getting into chat rooms until the next Harry Potter is released or the next edition of Halo.

4.   *Got Service? Get it on a Website*

How does your website affects your ability to attract and retain clients?

It is now almost unheard of to find a consulting, technology, or professional service business that does not have a web presence. But if you build it, will people come? And will they hand over their proverbial $20? It is all too common to hear service business leaders lament, "We've spent all this time and money on a website, and we have no idea if it is helping us generate clients or not." Essentially, they are wondering whether people are coming because the business built a website, and whether it is affecting their revenue stream. Over the last few years, we have identified five major effects that a website has on service business branding and service business marketing. By evaluating how your web presence stacks up, you can draw conclusions about how your website affects your ability to attract and retain clients.

Effect #1: First impressions
Nowadays, potential clients of service businesses form a good part of their initial opinion of a firm based on the firm's website. During their first website visit, prospects spend a minute or two quickly evaluating the following three questions:

- **How clearly does the management of this company communicate?** Based on the flow of content, clarity of content, and professional look of a website, potential clients develop a first impression of how well the people in the firm communicate.

- **How modern is this service firm?** Service business clients want to know that their service providers are actively engaged in staying current with new technologies and approaches to service delivery. If a service firm has a website that looks like it was built in 1998 with 1998 technologies for 1998 buyers, it raises questions in buyers' minds about how current the firm is.

- **Is this firm attentive to detail?** Mistakes such as bad grammar and typos, broken links, and out-of-date "current events" raise questions of quality. Website browsers, those who may become service customers, will ask themselves, "If their own website is full of errors, how good is their client work?" Essentially, they are asking themselves, "Is this firm up to my standards?"

Effect #2: Service specialty
After prospects form a general opinion of the quality of a service firm, if they have not dismissed the firm after forming their first impression, they then evaluate whether the specific service offerings apply to their needs. Clients look for specialties. For example, clients may want to know that a CPA firm has a specialty in "mid-market mergers and acquisitions" or "estate planning for clients with over $1 million in personal assets." If prospects find that the services are applicable to them, they may think, "This service specialty may be important to me soon. I'll have to remember this company."

Effect #3: Increased brand impressions
Many site viewers forget that a site exists because they visited only once. Like all advertising and marketing efforts, the creative piece and its core message must be seen and remembered. It does no good if the brand impression does not make, well, enough of an impression. Consider the following two points to make sure your brand and message are not forgotten:

- **Number of qualified site visitors:** When it comes to websites, if you build it, do not assume they will come. Marketing directed at driving qualified prospects to your site, search engine optimization (pay attention, because this is becoming more important as it is becoming more effective), and the overall searchability (from a technical perspective) of your site are important. Service firms can spend tens of thousands of dollars building their site, employ a webmaster to keep the content fresh and the site debugged, and then gain little marketing leverage from the site because there are too few qualified site visitors.

- **Power of brand impressions:** The more visitors return to your site because they find value in the content, the more affinity they are likely to have for you. A June 2004 study released by the Online Publishers Association (OPA) found as follows:

- *. . . 38% of "high affinity" visitors were "very or somewhat likely" to buy in the next three months. . . . Thirty-two percent of "low/medium affinity" users said they were "very or somewhat likely" to buy. The three measures used to create an affinity index are: a) the likelihood to recommend the site to* *a friend, b) satisfaction with site content, and c) whether the site is considered a "favorite" within its category.*

- The study builds on previous OPA research that indicated that users' affinity toward a website influenced their reaction to advertising on the site. Given this, ask yourself how much your site content gives viewers a reason to stay and a reason to return.

Effect #4: Service lead generation

Now assume that you have website visitors who believe that your service firm projects a high-quality image, that the service is applicable to them, and the site content is satisfactory. What do you do to convert them into buyers? You simply follow the tried-and-true direct marketing formula: You have already captured their attention, generated interest, and created a desire for your services. Now you have to get your prospects to take action. This action may be signing up for a consultation, registering for an event or webinar, inquiring about the service itself, becoming a newsletter subscriber, or requesting a white paper. Eliciting action from visitors is a necessary step to converting them from a website visitor into a live prospect.

Effect #5: Service loyalty

Let us assume you have a client discussing his great satisfaction with your services to a colleague. The colleague asks your client if your firm has a website. Your client may say, "Well, their website is a bit of a mess, but their services are great." They could also say, "Have a look at their website, you will be impressed with that as much as you will be impressed with their firm." The question you want to ask yourself is this: "Does our website support and strengthen the confidence our clients have in our firm, or is our website a liability that makes them question our professionalism and quality, thus limiting the number of colleagues they refer to us?"

This website visit is a critical component of the overall impression that a potential client forms about your service firm. As a result, it is essential for most service firms to:

- Build a website that creates a positive impression with appealing visuals and valuable content,
- Drive as many potential clients to that site as possible,
- And inspire them to engage your firm and become a loyal client for years to come.

Clearly, if you build it, they will not simply come. And if they come, but you do not build it right, you will not be seeing their $20.

5.   Be the Master of your Domain

Does your hosting company offer tech support?

Buying Domains
Curious who owns a website URL that you would like to own? Go to http://www.whois.sc and http://www.whois.org. These sites also show the deleted and expired domain names that are available.

Subdomains
A great way to get high ranking in the search engines is to get keywords in your domain name. Can't find a regular domain name with the keywords in it that are helpful to your business? Get a variation of the domain name and then add subdomains as needed. Your web host will advise you on making subdomains on your site.

Yahoo provides a decent FAQ on subdomains to help you learn more. http://help.yahoo.com/help/us/geo/subdomains

The cost for a domain should be no more than $8.95. Go Daddy is an excellent resource. Pay attention to who is the administrative contact under this domain name you purchase. Whoever is listed as the administrative contact will have tons of control over your website. Essentially, they would own your website. Not good.

Once you purchase your domain, you can stop and not do another thing and still hold onto that domain as long as you pay the yearly fee for that URL or domain name. When you're ready to activate the domain, you simply find a host and your host will give you instructions that involve the few simple steps to activate your domain.

The hosts I was mentioning are everywhere. If you're looking for help, Hart Creative Marketing, Inc. will set up hosting for you and assist in purchasing domains and subdomains.

(www.hartcreativemarketing.com)

You can bundle your hosting purchase in with your domain purchase if you find a hybrid host/domain provider. We can help you or, again, Go Daddy is a great resource.

My experience says stay away from any hosting company that doesn't offer technical support. And long before you sign up for their service make sure you test the ability to reach someone on the phone. Nothing is more painful than e-mail breakdown and not having a human being to help you work through your issue and resolve the problem. Of course, there are wider criteria to finding a solid host. Here are a few items to keep an eye out for:

- How many e-mail accounts will they supply? If you have 20 people or e-mail addresses you want to create, can they supply you that e-mail address volume?

- Do they have a dashboard of statistics you can quickly access?

- If you choose to open an ecommerce store, do they have "secured servers"?

- Are they forcing you into a long-term contract?

- Do you want audio or video on your site? Do they handle multimedia and CGI scripts?

- Limits on file transfers? Will you have to pay additional fees once you enroll?

- Backups? Do they have the capability to save your website content each evening while you're sleeping?

6. Website That "Woo" the Masses

Think of your home page as a giant magazine rack.

A great website begins with a clear understanding of your project goals. Is your site meant to increase sales? Streamline information distribution? Replace expensive offline processes? Entertain? Support existing offline channels? Extend your brand to international audiences? All of the above?

A great website also begins with a keen understanding of what your competitors are doing online. Are they e-commerce enabled? Is their site search engine optimized? Are they providing customers with extranet applications? Do they operate multiple sites to reach multiple audiences? Have they integrated CRM (customer relationship management) applications into their site?

We've talked about how to turn web visitors into your best customers by using inviting, influential, engaging e-mail/landing page opt-in lead generation strategies. Now, how do you create a new website or improve your existing website to increase your online success? Everyone can use great tips on writing and designing a website that gets results. Your website is your face to the world. It's unlike any other form of marketing or selling you'll ever do. If you want a website that people flock to, it needs to be rich in content and functionality.

Clarify your goals

Years ago, people built websites just to have a cyber presence. Today's websites can do much more. So first determine what you want your site to do. Do you want it to be an online brochure? Will it be educational? Will it be a sales vehicle? Are you doing e-marketing or e-commerce?

Determine key words and phrases

You must determine the words or phrases your audience will use to find your site. If an attorney uses "matrimonial attorney" and people search under "divorce lawyer," they won't find that attorney. If you're a money lender, for example, you may use "factoring," "asset-based loans," and "bridge loans." You can learn more in Chapter 10 (Search Engine Optimization) and understand why keywords have such a large impact on the number of visitors you'll have to your website.

Remember that first impressions are key

Always put the "good stuff" first. What is the good stuff? The goods are what is most relevant to the needs of the audience that is stopping in to your website. Relevance means connecting immediately with your target audience with content that speaks directly to their needs. The "good stuff" goes far beyond a website that matches the brand of your company in terms of aesthetics. Think of your homepage as a giant magazine rack. Your audience scans countless front covers of magazines not aware of the beauty of the cover of a magazine. They are simply searching for a connection to the content on a rack in the store on the web. Within 8 seconds, they'll decide to stay or look elsewhere, so make sure you capture their attention right away by meeting them on the bridge of relevance. You ought to feel some sense of gratitude you've managed to find a prospect visiting your website for the first time, so write the content for your prospects and customers.

Write for your audiences

Remember that your site should be about your audience, not just about you. You must understand and be able to convey "what's in it for them." Benefits and features work well. Look at the websites of your competitors to see how they tantalize (or frustrate).

Write for readability

Web audiences want instant information. Therefore, you must keep the text concise, often much shorter than its print equivalent. Here's how to give your audience the information they want quickly:

- Write headlines that give key information (Pattern your headlines after those you see in a newspaper)
- Limit paragraphs to eight lines of text
- Use bulleted lists
- Make effective use of white space and appropriate graphics

Go modular
Think about the content and how the average person will access your pages. Keep the topic and content of each page focused, making each page one complete thought or idea. This means that each page should be able to stand alone. People have different browsing styles, so they'll enter your website from different paths. Therefore, you should consider providing your key information on several pages of your site.

Link to other sites
No matter how great your content is, don't waste the most valuable feature of the web links. You've probably found that one of the best experiences you have on the web is the serendipity of stumbling upon a cool website you didn't know existed. When you provide useful links, your website becomes a valuable resource that your audience will return to, and recommend to others. Improve your search engine rankings by trading links with an alliance that places your link on their website.

Search engines give substantial bonus points when they see traffic coming from other websites that are related to your site. Bottom line, it's not just link sharing that's key, it's having a commonality (similar keywords seen on the page) that reflect the keywords that are found on the shared site. More on search engines and marketing can be found in Chapters 8 and 9.

Build in tracking
You must be able to quantify the return on investment (ROI) of your website by measuring the activity of visitors, e-marketing, e-mails, faxes, and phone calls. It is critical to know who visits your site and how often.

Publicize your site
What good is your wonderful site if people don't know it exists or how to find it? Here are some ways to publicize your site after it's published:

- Include the URL on your letterhead, business cards, and e-newsletters (some people print out e-newsletters and distribute them).
- Add the URL to the signature portion of all your e-mail messages.
- Post it to appropriate newsgroups.
- Send out a press release, if that's appropriate for your business.

Keep your site current
A static site is a boring site. A static site may work for some businesses, but you want to give people a reason to return. A good way to keep your site current is to include new links, industry tips

and trends, and any other information your audience will find useful.

Website Taboos
There are a number of reasons that websites aren't successful. Here are just a few:

- **Lack of key words:** You must have the key words people will use to search for your site. Otherwise, they won't know you're there. These words must be peppered throughout the site because you may not know where people enter.

- **Bleeding-edge technology:** Your site isn't New York City's Times Square. Don't use images that have an overpowering effect on the human peripheral vision just because you can. That's akin to generating documents that look like circus posters just because you have a word processor. Include only what you need and what's appropriate for your business.

- **Hard-to-read colors:** People still use black backgrounds with yellow lettering, or something equally awful. Use appropriate, readable colors.

- **Outdated information:** Keep your site current. You need a web gardener to weed your web garden and replant new flowers. An outdated site is the sign of an outdated company.

- **Long downloads:** Human factors guidelines show that audiences lose interest after 8 seconds and, despite the growing popularity of high-speed internet, many people still use dial-up modems, so download time may be a factor for your audience.

International Websites
Contrary to popular belief, the United States doesn't own the internet, and as internet access grows across the globe, so do translation and download problems. Here are some guidelines to help meet the needs of a worldwide audience:

- **Work with a translator:** If the site is to be translated, identify the languages. Send text, menus, and entries to the translator to learn of potential problems. For example, in other languages, nouns may not have similar conventions and many words and phrases we typically use may be offensive.

- **Be aware of download time:** There are many parts of the world that have slow modems with internet access billed by the minute. Users in these areas (and some are right here in the United States) will visit sites that are quick to download.

- **Site must be printable:** There are also parts of the world where internet access is very expensive and users often share computers. People print out websites and distribute hard copy pages.

7.   *Your Site: Build Up or Implode*

What is your "measurable return"?

If a website redesign is what you're striving for, here's a quick guide to make your business case. The phrase that pays in these tight-fisted times is "measurable return," and we're getting more and more requests from corporate marketers to help them make the return on investment (ROI) case before they can earmark a redesign budget. Let's make a business case for a site redesign.

Method 1: The devil is in the data
Sure, we can gripe all the way to 2030 that the web channel gets held to an unjustly high standard for performance measurement, but complaining isn't going to get us our redesign any faster. So let's make the best of what the web does well: It delivers real numbers.

Start with your overall corporate marketing budget. Chances are it's bigger next year. That fact alone should create some urgency around the website. When spending increases in other channels, traffic to the website surges (that's your URL on your marketing materials, after all), and greeting all those new visitors with a less-than-optimal site is like throwing good money after bad.

Some basic analysis of your site traffic data will help you decide how much more money gets left on the table when marketing spending goes up. How much of your traffic abandons the site from the homepage alone? What percentage of your overall traffic fulfills valuable actions (e.g., making a purchase, filling out a lead form)?
Of course, finding your soft spots is only half the battle. In order to calculate increased return on your overall marketing investment, you need to project a reasonable degree of improvement, and that can be tricky. You have a few options. One is to seek the input of an interactive agency (shameless plug for Hart Creative Marketing, Inc.'s team of professionals hungry to help you improve your site and your sales) or a data aggregator like Forrester or Jupiter. Chances are they've seen enough data on soft spots like yours to project accurately what improvements will accomplish.

The other option is to run a few head-to-head tests on the live site. You can substitute an alternate page in a single critical spot on your site, for instance, and use the percentage improvement as a leading indicator of what overall site enhancements can accomplish. A single powerful instance of actual improvement can be the centerpiece of your business case.

Method 2: Making headcount count
Surveys of projected IT (information technology) spending for next year show that tools designed to improve workflow are at the top of everybody's wish list. The must-have item is portal technology, which enables things like centralized document distribution and multiple access levels for employee intranets and customer extranets. Next in line is content management software, which gives nontechnical users the ability to update website content.

These tools are getting serious buzz right now in part because the licensing prices have dropped faster than a post-Christmas sale on an inflatable Santa. For that reason alone, any company contemplating a redesign needs to consider adding workflow tools to the equation. Calculating the ROI on such a tool is relatively easy because it's meant to replace work your company is already doing. If it takes six times as long to maintain your site with manual updates, or if employees use 400 hours/year of the HR department's time requesting information that could be posted on an intranet, then the resultant headcount savings is the core of your business case.

Method 3: Making the truth hurt
For Scrooge, it took visits from three spirits to spook him enough to pry open his purse strings. For even the most tight-fisted corporate budget-holder, eight to ten real-life site users ought to do the job. Make your stubborn hold-outs attend a usability lab, in which representative users try to complete basic tasks on the site and give you a blow-by-blow of what goes wrong for them.

In our experience, there is nothing quite so sobering or illuminating as hearing it straight from the user. But the usability lab is not just for shock effect. When done properly by an experienced information architect, a usability lab yields precise, usable data on what's not working and how to fix it. Of course, being able to lace your business case with cries of pain from frustrated users doesn't hurt either.

A usability lab requires more of an upfront investment than Method 1, but it also yields a deeper data set. As a general rule, consider that just 5 to 10% of your web marketing budget set aside for user testing will always pay itself back in performance, often several times over.

Method 4: The pilot project

Sometimes our New Year's resolutions reach too far, like when you resolve to run a marathon, and by May you're using the treadmill for a clothes hanger. Better to set your sites a little lower and take on something realistic. This has become something of a trend in web development: doing a partial redesign and using the results to make a case for full redesign down the road.

For most corporate websites, there are plenty of opportunities to do this without creating serious discontinuity in the user experience. Often a single "flagship" product site under a corporate umbrella gets redesigned, or a "micro-site" is developed to handle traffic from a campaign. In the latter case, the conversion performance of the micro-site is compared to that of the original site in order to calculate potential gains from a redesign.

Checklists

Write 3 sentences you can use to entice your website reader.

_____

_____

_____

Describe your organization's personality

_____

_____

_____

List 5 discussion boards you can use to direct traffic to your website.

_____

_____

_____

_____

_____

List at least 3 domain and sub-domain names you can use for your web prescence.

_____

_____

_____

List at least 8 goals for your website.

_____

_____

_____

_____

_____

_____

_____

_____

Name 5 things that are important for your hosting company to provide.

_____

_____

_____

_____

_____

Define your website budget for the next 3 years. Remember that planning up-front will help you to spend less as your site grows.

_____

_____

_____

_____

_____

_____

_____

_____

How will you be testing your site before it becomes live?

_____

_____

_____

_____

_____

_____

_____

_____

_____

NOTES

3. Email Quality Assurance

1.   *Seriously, Dude, Where's My Email*

What pops into your mind first?

Think about the e-mail you receive on any given day. What pops into your mind first? If you're like most people online today, you think about all of the "spam"—the unsolicited e-mails touting get-rich-quick schemes, questionable herbal remedies, and other shaky offers that regularly fill your inbox. This chapter is filled with spam fighting solutions.

This chapter will include information on e-mail blocking, e-mail filters, and false positives. I'll define the issues and terms, explain what industry experts are doing on your behalf, and tell you what you can do to make sure your permission-based
e-mails get through to their intended recipients.

You can bet there are boardrooms all over the country filled with frustrated executives, more specifically the Internet Service Providers (ISPs), wondering how many more months it will take to stop the spam flowing into their e-mail inboxes. My first question is always, where is your spam filter? There are plenty on the market that are worth the nominal charge to stop spam.

But despite all of the efforts to decrease spam, a foolproof solution has not yet been created. And, as a result of current e-mail blocking and filtering techniques, a lot of legitimate permission-based e-mail is being blocked as well. In the industry, we call this a "false-positive."

"On average, 30% of legitimate commercial e-mail does not make it to the intended inbox," according to Assurance Systems.

So, what do "false positives" mean to you?
If you were one of the early admission applicants to Harvard University eagerly awaiting e-mail notification of your acceptance or rejection last December, you could have been among 100 of those applicants who never received word. All because Harvard e-mails were inadvertently flagged as junk mail and blocked by AOL.

And, to quote Trevor Hughes, Executive Director of The Network Advertising Initiative: "If you're expecting a gift certificate from an online bookstore or a city meeting notice, you may never see it due to the blacklists and filters that are currently in place. Or a message to your accountant may bounce, if someone has put the server that handles your company's e-mail on its blacklist. A message from a long lost high school buddy may be filtered if he uses too many exclamation marks."

Sounds grim, huh? It really isn't. There's light at the end of the tunnel.

Spam is universally recognized as an industry-wide crisis on the internet and experts representing all areas of knowledge are working together like never before to come up with a solution.

So what are the experts doing? Well, the National Advertising Initiative's E-mail Service Provider Coalition, which can be found at www.networkadvertising.org, is a group comprised of companies that provide e-mail services to the full spectrum of the marketplace. The coalition's goal is to provide solutions to the spam problem and to protect the appropriate use of e-mail as a business and marketing communications tool.

2.   *Getting Past the Spam Filters*

> If some of your e-mail is being blocked, know that you're not alone.

What type of content will fly or dies in the spam filter? What can you do to make sure your permission-based e-mail gets through? If your e-mail is being blocked at a particular company or ISP, ask your subscribers to help by contacting their postmaster and requesting to have your e-mail address unblocked.

If your e-mail is being filtered, check your "from" line, subject line, and e-mail copy and avoid using keywords or format style that might look like spam or be suspicious to a content-based spam filter:

- ALL CAPITAL LETTERS
- Excessive punctuation!!!!
- Excessive use of "click here," $$, and other symbols
- The words free, guarantee, spam, credit card, sex, etc.
- Redundant unsubscribe instructions

Finally, if some of your e-mail is being blocked, know that you're not alone. If you have the right vendor, know that you are in good hands. Why? Because a reputable e-mail service provider:

- Delivers your e-mails using the proper protocols

- Maintains strong permission policies and an active anti-blocking team working on your behalf

- Develops relationships with ISPs and is white listed to ensure their customers' permission-based e-mail gets through

- Provides reports and bounce management and helps you stay on top of current best practices, like including a failsafe one-click unsubscribe link in every e-mail

- Is at the forefront of the industry, protecting the appropriate use of e-mail as a business and marketing communications tool through its involvement in organizations like the ones listed above

And, if a problem does arise, a good e-mail service provider gets more attention than you could ever get on your own. In the meantime, here is a glossary of terms to add to your repertoire:

- **E-mail Blocking** E-mail blocking occurs when the receiving e-mail server (e.g., Yahoo, AOL, Hotmail) prevents an inbound e-mail from reaching the inbox of the intended recipient. Most of the time the sender of the e-mail receives a "bounce" message notifying the sender that their e-mail has been blocked.

- **Filters** "Filtering" is a technique used to block e-mail based on the content in the "from" line, subject line, or body copy of an e-mail. Filtering software searches for keywords and other indicators that identify the e-mail as potential spam. This type of blocking searches each individual e-mail.

- **False Positive** A false positive occurs when a legitimate permission-based e-mail is incorrectly filtered or blocked as spam.

- **Blacklist** It is common for an ISP to use a blacklist to determine which e-mails should be blocked. Blacklists contain lists of domains or IP addresses of known and suspected spammers. (Your IP address is your machine's unique online identifying number, analogous to your phone number.) Unfortunately, these blacklists also contain many legitimate e-mail service providers. Just a few spam complaints can land an e-mail service provider or IP address on a blacklist despite the fact that the ratio of complaints to volume of e-mail sent is extremely low.

- **White list** A white list is the opposite of a blacklist. Instead of listing IP addresses to block, a white list includes IP addresses that have been approved to deliver e-mail despite blocking measures. It is common practice for ISPs to maintain both a blacklist and a white list. When e-mail service providers, like any e-mail sending company you are using to send e-mails, say they are "white listed" it means that their IP addresses are on a specific ISP's white list and they are confident that e-mails sent using their service will be delivered.

3. *That's Not Spam – I Want That Email*

Make sure you reduce any risk of your e-mails not reaching the recipient

Sending Outbound E-mails
You will want to make sure you reduce any risk of your e-mails not reaching the recipient. I highly recommend you place this format of a typical header disclaimer at the top of each e-mail when sending your campaigns.

"Be sure to add this e-mail address:
(hart@hartcreativemarketing.com)

To ensure you receive future mailings. If you are unable to view this message please go here:
 www.webaddress.com/emailmessage.html"

The point is to reinforce to your audience that they may have their e-mail settings adjusted to block anyone who has not been placed in the "accept e-mails from this person" folder. Each e-mail client has a set of actions available that are needed to allow any one recipient to enter the inbox. Once you block a sender from reaching you, you would need to add the e-mail address of the person you wish to allow into your inbox.

Receiving Inbound E-mails
To ensure you're receiving e-mails from those you want to, and you're using one of these spam enhanced e-mail delivery systems to send your e-mail, like Outlook, simply follow the instructions you find from this link.

http://www.hartcreativemarketing.com/quicktips/images/safe-sender.pdf

The procedure will allow you to receive e-mails securely and without interruption from those on your trusted list. Feel free to steal my PDF document and brand it with your company's brand. Share it with your e-mail recipients to help them add you to their senders list so your e-mails reach their destination.

Many e-mail providers have "spam" or "junk" functions that will automatically delete or block e-mails that you report as "spam" or "junk." Hitting these buttons may prevent you from receiving e-mail from all members who contact you—not just the individual e-mail that you may not wish to view. For best results, avoid using these functions with any e-mail sender from whom you wish to receive communications.

If your e-mail looks distorted or if the links within the e-mail do not work, your
e-mail provider may be automatically sending e-mails to your inbox with the images and links deliberately turned off. Many e-mail providers provide functions that allow you to see images and links in your e-mail; it's often just a matter of hitting a button or two. Contact your e-mail provider for assistance on allowing images and links to display in your e-mail.

4. *The Facts About Confirmed Opt-In*

So, what is a "confirmed opt-in"?

To set the record straight, there is no set standard for "proof" of opt-in. Single opt-in or double opt-in is best. I'll explain the differences between the two opt-in types in a moment. The legal penalties are stiff for those that choose to ignore the consequences for not keeping clean e-mail database records. Although the United States is not nearly as strict as the United Kingdom, it is militant enough to keep all of us on our toes in a world of e-mail inbox corruption. The misuse and abuse of e-mails has forced the government to take action against those who essentially see the e-mail channel as the most cost-effective means of marketing. Hard to believe an e-mail soliciting the enlargement of a particular appendage can still find buyers.

When is it going to end? Not anytime soon. The only logical reason these spam e-mails reach their destination, day in and day, out is that recipients still buy from these ridiculous e-mail ads. The effect of this mayhem should have you on high alert when you even start to think about sending e-mail campaigns.

If for some reason you're questioned by the government or your ISP (Internet Service Provider), you'll need to show reasonable data that might include the date and time an e-mail address was collected or the form on which the address was collected. Yes, the form found online or the paperwork you gathered offline to procure that specific name and e-mail address. More advanced protection, in case you come under scrutiny, would be to have the source code/name/form identifier and URL of your form used to collect your recipient's contact data. Having an archived version of the form with the IP address of the form registrant for reference after it's been taken down from the web will also help. It's not mandatory, but, the more of an arsenal you have to fight with in a court of law, the more likely you can avoid getting blasted by as little as one individual who has plenty of time on his or her hands to prove you are guilty of spamming. This isn't meant to scare you. Instead, see this as a roadmap that will decrease your liability and save you a ton of grief.

If you're a permission-based e-mail marketer independently sending out your e-mail campaigns, or you outsource your e-marketing, you need to remain diligent in your efforts to manage your lists according to best practices.

So, what is a "confirmed opt-in"? It's the most rigorous method of obtaining permission to send e-mail campaigns. It's generated a bit of a buzz in the e-mail marketing world. What the heck does confirmed opt-in mean? And is it for you? Well, first let's define the terms.

Single Opt-In (with a subscriber acknowledgment e-mail) is the most widely accepted and routinely used method of obtaining e-mail addresses and permission. A single opt-in list is created by inviting visitors and customers to subscribe to your e-mail list. When you use a signup tag on your website, a message immediately goes out to the subscriber acknowledging the subscription. This message should reiterate what the subscriber has signed up for, and provide an immediate way for the subscriber to edit his or her interests or opt out.

Confirmed Opt-In (a.k.a. double opt-in) is a more stringent method of obtaining permission to send e-mail campaigns. Confirmed opt-in adds another step to the opt-in process. It requires the subscriber to respond to a confirmation e-mail, either by clicking on a confirmation link or by replying to the e-mail to confirm the subscription. Only those subscribers who take this additional step are added to your list.

ISPs and corporations are now doing everything they can to stem the tide of spam flowing into their employees' e-mail inboxes. Without a foolproof solution to turn to, some ISPs, like Road Runner (@rr.com e-mail addresses), now require confirmed opt-in for e-mail delivery. They do this because the subscription tracking capabilities associated with confirmed opt-in can help them differentiate legitimate commercial e-mail from spam and protect their customers from receiving spam.

The advantages of confirmed opt-in
In a nutshell, confirmed opt-in ensures that those who are receiving your e-mail want to receive it. It can protect you against spam accusations and it allows for e-mail delivery to ISPs, like Road Runner, that require confirmed opt-in for successful e-mail delivery.

The confirmed opt-in method prevents:
- E-mail address collection without permission
- Accidental subscription due to e-mail address typos
- Subscriptions made by an unauthorized third party

The disadvantages of confirmed opt-in

The majority of permission e-mail marketers do not use confirmed opt-in. So, most subscribers to an e-mail list are not accustomed to confirming their subscriptions. As a result, confirmation messages are unexpected and largely disregarded.

Most accounts see confirm rates of only 30 to 60% of their subscribers. And, with confirmed opt-in, there's no going back. Subscribers who do not respond to your confirmation e-mail are removed from your list and cannot be e-mailed to again. Ouch, that hurts.

Confirmed opt-in is not for everyone

For most lists I do not recommend confirmed opt-in at this time, primarily because of poor consumer response and adoption, but also because confirmed opt-in is not today's industry standard. If you have collected e-mail addresses and permission from your subscribers in good faith and according to e-mail marketing best practices, if you have high-quality relationships with your subscriber base, high opens and click-throughs, low abuse complaints, and a low unsubscribe rate, applying confirmed opt-in is an unnecessary risk to your existing list.

If, however, you have a tech savvy audience that will be receptive and responsive to confirmation e-mails, or if you have a high percentage of subscribers whose ISPs require confirmed opt-in for e-mail delivery, and/or if fully informed of the advantages and disadvantages, you want to adopt the most stringent level of permission when building and mailing to your e-mail list, you may choose to use confirmed opt-in.

If so, my advice is to start small. Here are some options:

- Test a small portion of your list to see the response before you apply confirmed opt-in to your entire list. This way, you can test your own audience and know what to expect before taking the plunge. It could be a Nestea® plunge (Ahhh!), or a nosedive (Ouch!).

- Consider confirming only those e-mail addresses on your list that require confirmed opt-in for e-mail delivery. Without confirmed opt-in, you won't be able to reach those addresses anyway, so no risk there, right? Finally, you may choose to confirm only new subscribers. While your new subscribers will be fewer in number, you will be building a clean list with low complaint rates.

5.   *Take Me Off Your List*

Something I often run into are dedicated e-mail "contritionists": folks who like to write apologetic things like this in their e-mail outreach: *We know you receive a lot of unwanted e-mail, and we want you to know that we value your privacy. We hate spam as much as you do, but we wanted to tell you about. . . .*

You know the rest. I don't call that e-mail marketing, I call it "whimper marketing," and I think it's totally unnecessary. In fact, if you're engaged in marketing and you feel a need to apologize for it, stop marketing. Stand tall with you chin up because you send out direct e-mail and you're proud of it. You know it's not spam. You know there's a difference between porn and what you do, between cheap mortgages and what you do, between generic Viagra and what you do. Between you and that tragic third-world widow who just needs you to launder a billion dollars for her. You're not spamming. You're marketing. Spam is bad. Marketing is good. And you're using a respectable medium to send a respectable message of value to people who can benefit from it.

Of course, if you are spamming, if you are one of those who send me the same messages five times a day for free software and big money opportunities stuffing envelopes, there's no hope for you anyway and you should stop reading this and go add some more exclamation points to your outbound e-mails. I send out e-mail. I have a newsletter. You know how I get people to subscribe? I don't wait for them to opt-in. My marketplace consists of C-level people and the people who influence them. Generally speaking, they don't opt-in to anything. They have no time to spend on the web. I value and appreciate the people who opt-in to my newsletter, but I also realize that they are not likely to be hiring me. It's their bosses' bosses who do that. I find the names of the people I want to reach, I determine what their e-mail addresses are, and I reach out to them.

First, I send them an e-mail and ask if I can send my newsletter, and then I send it to them every other week like clockwork. A few say no, but it's a very few. The rest say yes because they recognize from the first e-mail that I'm not sending them junk. I let them know that the newsletter contains articles very much like those I write on my website, point them to my archives so they can taste the goods, and so on. And, by the way, there's a real craft to getting e-mails read. It has little to do with sizzling headlines and a lot to do with talking to a marketplace about things the marketplace wants to be talked to about. But that's a whole other matter.

And they read those newsletters when they arrive. Sure, some must block them. And some certainly dump them when they see my name.

But something along the lines of 70% read them, and I'm satisfied with that. And I do this without going on about spam and privacy and cluttered inboxes and so on. If they don't want to receive it, they will tell me so. If they don't like what they're receiving, they'll ask me not to send it anymore and I won't. Besides, most of them are likely e-mail marketers as well, so we're compatriots, not combatants. I know it's not spam, so I see no reason to bring the issue up. And my list knows it, too, and doesn't need to be reassured. We get along just fine without my apologizing for wanting to sell them something.

6.   *In-House Vs. Rental Lists*

E-mail as a profit center.

Most people I run into fail to see e-mail as a profit center and even more, sadly deny themselves one of the most amazing business growth opportunities: ongoing e-mail communications with an in-house list. First, let me explain the difference between an in-house list and a rental list.

In-house or house lists, your database of permission-based recipients, are generally used for retention, newsletters, etc. You find a lower cost per contact and acquisition. Plus, you're limited only by what you've collected about customers and your ability to keep them engaged.

A typical rental list campaign is usually 4000–5000 names minimum. Your cost per thousand names, known as CPM is around $300 to $500. Renting a list is not good for all industries and titles. A specific niche, such as HR directors at a firm with $100 million-plus revenue, in one geographic area will cost much more than 200,000 general consumers across the nation.

Most often, a rental list is used to send an offer "blind" to people who have agreed to receive third party offers. Opt-in is key here. The sole objective should be to collect a name for future use. Remember, the list is not yours. You're renting the list and have a one-time opportunity, when the list manager sends your e-mail campaign to incite a recipient to submit his or her e-mail address.

The concept of renting a list, sending a campaign to that list of names, and only expecting them to buy from you is not enough. Think of potential revenue down the road from some of those e-mail recipients that may be willing to give you their
e-mail address. Don't underestimate what great marketers have already adopted in their e-mail strategy.

The method I encourage you to adopt is to always view your rental list as a means of lead generation. There will be plenty of people who will not buy from you now and could still end up your most loyal customer. You must accept the hard, cold facts that consumers today are more cautious than ever about opening e-mail, and taking the time to offer up education on your products or services is a smart way to go. Why? If I receive your e-mail from a list manager (e.g., Equifax) and I'm not ready to buy, give me an alternative to deleting your e-mail. Educate me or offer me a value to join your list. A value may be a free webinar, a free white paper, a promotional offer; some relevant content that encourages me to sign up to your in-house list. This bridge between a rental list and the organic growth of your in-house list may be one of the best kept secrets in e-mail marketing today.

A few rules to the game of renting a list

Be very careful when choosing an e-mail rental vendor. Make sure when seeking a list broker/provider that you request references to call. Calling on an internet marketer you can trust to help you find a quality list vendor is critical. Having a company you recognize as credible is key in getting a truthful testimony of the level of return this referral gained from the list provider you're about to buy a list from. They will have the experience to see any weaknesses in relationship to where the vendor located the list you want to rent, if they have a respectful track record, and if their rates are competitive.

No legitimate rental list provider will allow you to see the list of e-mail addresses, as opposed to a direct mail list, which you usually have rights to use for the duration of one year. If you're purchasing an e-mail list, beware. Most lists you buy will lead you down SPAM alley as the list quite possibly has been sold many times over. You may have found a great price for a million e-mail addresses; however, your exposure to penalties from the government for not being compliant with the CAN-SPAM Act is a dangerous tightrope walk to balance. Do not buy a list, only rent.

When you do choose a vendor and you make the purchase, remember you do not own the list. The vendor has the relationship with the list owner and brokers with you to help you deliver your e-mail message to a specific database of potential customers.

The e-mail creative content will need to be delivered to the list vendor, who deploys the message to the database of e-mail addresses you rented. You have only one shot to touch the audience with your message—unlike postal address lists, which you own and to which you can repeatedly send marketing messages. Remember, your sole objective is to capture the recipient's e-mail address so you can begin a direct relationship with the individual who was e-mailed from the vendor's rental list. So, you rent the list, they send your message, recipients come to your website from the e-mail message and you capture their contact information to help you make a sale, and you grow your own community of opt-in permission-based recipients to whom you can market your services for years to come.

An important detail is the test e-mail, which the vendor should send to you prior to the e-mail's official day and time of delivery to the list of rented e-mail addresses. You'll want to be sure the test e-mail the vendor sends is delivered directly to your inbox, not to a bulk junk folder. If you have followed the rules for creating an e-mail that has been formatted properly—meaning no spam-like headlines and code inside the HTML message is compliant—it will be delivered to your inbox. Do not approve any campaign if the test e-mail message ends up in your bulk folder. Ask your web designer to review your e-mail message to meet a level of quality that keeps you out of the junk folder and in the inboxes of an audience ready to welcome your e-mail message. Those are the people who opted in to receive information from your list rental vendor and you need to make sure your e-mail will reach them. I suggest you deliver the code source of the HTML to the list vendor and instruct the vendor to deliver your e-mail without adjusting the code.

How to deliver the code properly?
You can open your e-mail on a web browser, right click with your mouse, highlight view source, then copy and paste code into a "Notepad" file. Save as the name you wish and send that file to your rental list provider.

One more point: Most rental list vendors will add tracking code to the e-mail message to determine who viewed your e-mail and who clicked through to your website or landing page. Although this tracking feature loaded into your code is great, most vendors will attach the code *inside your code* and in the process will compromise the code you delivered. That's why over the years we've learned to demand the rental list vendor be very aware that they not adjust any of the HTML code that we worked so hard to bring up to SPAM and inbox filter requirements. Insist on the same protection for your code.

7.   *Eleven Tips for Successful Opt-In*

> Do you keep in touch with your current and previous clients?

Do you keep in touch with your current and previous clients? Are you building an e-mail list of your potential customers? What about those prospects that you've been meaning to contact. Do you feel a little awkward cold-calling them? Here are some ideas for successful e-mail newsletters and campaigns:

1. Do not purchase, trade, or borrow an e-mail list.
E-mail sent to people who have not specifically requested to receive your mailings is almost always regarded as spam. Sure, I see people

every day sending e-mails to a list that is not opt-in with impressive results. Of course, it's risky. If you do this, it's a numbers game and may be littered with SPAM complainers who will most likely contact their ISP to make sure they're aware your e-mail was not permission based.

2. Make signing up and unsubscribing easy and visible.
Add a signup form to your website homepage or a link to it and ask your customers whether they would like to sign up when you speak with them in person. You may want to ask subscribers only for their e-mail address, first and last name, and one or two other questions such as their interests. This will allow you to target future mailings.

3. Link to your privacy policy.
Place a link to your privacy policy near your list signup form. Your policy should describe how you handle the information you collect and how people can contact you in case they have any concerns or questions. There are plenty of privacy policies across the web that you can tailor to your own company's policies and regulations.

4. Send a welcome message to each new subscriber.
Once someone subscribes, send a welcome message immediately. Include a description of what they will receive and how frequently, and how to unsubscribe. This step is often overlooked and if missed can lead to your getting blamed for spamming. By sending the welcome message immediately after they sign up, you're more likely to be remembered by the recipient when you e-mail them again in 30 days.

5. Keep accurate signup records.
Sometimes, you or your Internet Service Provider (ISP) will get a spam complaint from someone who forgot they subscribed to your list requesting to receive your content. Keep accurate records that include the date and website and e-mail address from which they signed up.

Worst case scenario? If you end up in the inbox of a forgetful individual who had no reminder they signed up, you may have to prove you're spam compliant. Meaning, it's not about what you know, it's about the memory of the recipient. The only protection you have against an angry e-mail recipient is a digital stamp showing he or she subscribed on such and such a date. If the subscriber simply forgot he or she subscribed to your list and feels you're spamming, you're safe, but only with the proof of subscription.

6. Ask your members to opt-in again for older lists.
If you have not sent a mailing for a while, ask subscribers to indicate that they want to remain on your list by sending you an e-mail, clicking a link, or visiting a website.

7. Remind people that they subscribed.
Include a standard heading each time you send a message. A short note such as "Thank you for subscribing to our newsletter, Mary" will remind recipients that they requested your mailings. Plus, it shows gratitude in the e-mail space that, after all, is in short supply of integrity.

8. Avoid certain terms: subject line and message text.
If your message contains words frequently used by spammers, people will delete it and possibly file a spam complaint. ISPs often filter e-mails with suspicious subject lines. Also note that it's illegal to use deceptive or misleading ones.

9. Include your physical address and phone number.
Put your phone number and postal mailing address in your message. This allows readers to contact you to place an order or inquire about your services. In addition, new federal legislation *requires* physical addresses on commercial e-mail messages.

10. Send your mailings regularly.
Keep in touch with your subscribers frequently so they don't forget they signed up to receive your mailings. They will begin to anticipate your messages if you adhere to a schedule.

11. Reply promptly to each inquiry or complaint.
When you receive an inquiry or a spam complaint, respond to it as soon as possible. Always include the subscriber's signup information with your response. Following these simple suggestions will help you retain your subscriber base, which is fundamental for a thriving permission-based e-newsletter or outreach campaign.

Having your own opt-in permission-based e-newsletter might be the answer. It is one of the most effective marketing tools you can use, because it is fast, personal, and inexpensive.

Many small businesses are using e-newsletters to introduce themselves to new customers and to communicate with existing ones. By sending useful information on a regular basis, you maintain constant contact without being annoying. In addition, an e-mail newsletter can enhance your credibility and increase sales.

8.   *Email Content and Filtering Rules*

> The impact of new anti-spam legislation should also be kept in mind at all times.

Delivering marketing e-mails to a customer database is no longer a simple matter of hitting the send button. Major ISPs expect owners of e-mail marketing lists to follow certain rules of good conduct, and they remove those that don't comply so that noncompliant messages don't reach the intended recipients. This topic is specifically for companies who choose to send mass e-mail campaigns through their ISP's servers. Many outsource to ESPs (e-mail service providers) to avoid meeting compliance.

The impact of new anti-spam legislation should also be kept in mind. In an ideal world, keeping up to date with all of these rules wouldn't be a marketer's job. This is a discipline that is best outsourced to a special e-mail vendor. However, if you are in a position where you need to manage this aspect of e-mail delivery yourself, here are some basic rules to follow:

Publish your sender policy framework (SPF) records.
An SPF record verifies the legitimacy of your messages to receiving e-mail servers. I also recommend that you publish your SPF records for your corporate e-mail servers to protect your mail systems from being spoofed or forged, a step that will help to protect the integrity of your brand.

Learn more about why accreditation and reputation are necessary at: http://spf.pobox.com/aspen.html

How do you publish your SPF? You need to ask whoever in your organization is responsible for maintaining your DNS (Domain Name System) records and corporate e-mail servers to help you publish the SPF. They can create your SPF record using SPF Wizard software available from the aforementioned website. The final step in publishing your SPF record is to paste the record created by the SPF Wizard software into your zone file.

Afterward, test the implementation by going here: www.dnsstuff.com/pages/spf.htm

To do so, you will need to know your sender address (for example, newsletter@mail.domain.biz) and the sender IP address (ask your e-mail vendor or IT department for help).

Complying with CAN-SPAM
Complying with the Controlling the Assault of Non-Solicited Pornography and Marketing Act of 2003 (or CAN-SPAM) is relatively easy. Your e-mails should contain a valid return address, your physical address should be clearly displayed, and your branding should be prominent in the message and e-mail domain name.

In addition, an e-mail should clearly identify the sender and the subject matter at the beginning of the communication. All commercial e-mail (except for billing purposes) must provide consumers with an unsubscribe option. The removal process must take place within 10 business days. The unsubscribe mechanism must be available for 30 days.

You should also avoid gathering e-mail addresses for your lists through unscrupulous methods such as harvesting them from websites using automated tools without consumer consent. And do not sell your e-mail lists to third parties without providing notice to your customers and giving them the opportunity to be removed from the database you sell.

All commercial e-mail should contain your privacy policy, either within the body of the e-mail or via a link.

Filtering
An ISP may block your e-mails if your IP address is on a DNS block list, if the recipients of your messages are not valid users, or if your connecting host isn't authorized to send mail from its domain.

IP addresses that become known for sending out a lot of spam tend to end up on blacklists, and many ISPs will not deliver messages from those addresses to their customers.

When a listed IP address meets certain criteria laid out by the operator of the block list, it can be removed from the list. It is easy to be blacklisted but difficult to be removed from block lists, especially if you do not even know at which source your IP address is being blocked. The best way to avoid this is to follow the basic principles outlined above.

The role of e-mail vendors
Outsourcing the functions above to a specialist saves time and frees up marketers to focus on their core functions. Choose an e-mail provider that is on top of all the latest developments that affect the delivery of marketing e-mails, including sender policy framework (SPF), sender ID, spam legislation, and ISP filters.

The e-mail vendor should also have strong working relationships with the major ISPs to ensure that your e-mail IP address is not on the list of blocked addresses (and to negotiate for speedy unblocking if it gets blocked) and keep up to date with the changing rules ISPs use for filtering systems to make sure that your e-mails do reach end users.

9.   Can-SPAM Compliance

What pops into your mind first?

On January 1, 2004, commercial e-mail became a federally regulated activity thanks to the CAN-SPAM Act. This legislation, which became significantly more potent in the course of its final revision in December 2003, provides for both civil and criminal liability for wrongdoers.

Although targeted at those whose activities were already questionable under existing laws, the CAN-SPAM Act may ensnare legitimate businesses as well, especially small businesses with no compliance experience. Every law has its first fall guy. It's only a matter of time before CNN broadcasts the first CAN-SPAM "perp walk."

For this reason, companies large and small must establish compliance programs and train their employees, especially those in sales and marketing. The trick to compliance is in interpreting the law as conservatively as possible, since no courts have yet heard a case. The following will help get you started:

Consent: good to have, but not a free pass
Earlier versions of CAN-SPAM applied primarily to unsolicited commercial e-mail, but the final version of the law applies to all commercial e-mail. Furthermore, the law recognizes only one form of consent, "affirmative consent" (it used to also recognize "implied consent"). Although obtaining affirmative consent enables you to bypass some of the law's requirements, no one knows how far such consent extends.

For example, suppose you publish a monthly e-newsletter that uses a double opt-in subscription process. Under the law, you likely have the affirmative consent of your subscribers to send them your newsletter every month. But what if you decide to increase the frequency to biweekly? Or what if you also periodically send standalone promotional messages to the same subscribers?

Until a court or the FTC addresses the scope of affirmative consent, take a conservative approach. Treat all of your company's commercial e-mail as unsolicited, and make sure it complies with *all* of the law's requirements.

Eight not-so-simple rules for CAN-SPAM compliant e-mail
Complying with the CAN-SPAM Act with respect to your lists entails adhering to the eight rules discussed below. As you read through these rules, keep in mind that just one e-mail message can trigger a CAN-SPAM violation. Therefore, you should apply these rules not only to your bulk distributions but also to individual solicitations sent by your salespeople.

1. Staying out of prison
As bad as paying a civil fine of $250 per noncompliant e-mail message may sound, going to prison is considerably worse. Therefore, it is absolutely essential to make sure that no one at your company engages in any of the activities that the

CAN-SPAM Act has criminalized:

- Intentionally sending commercial e-mail from a foreign or domestic computer that you do not have authorization to use.

- Using a foreign or domestic computer to "relay or retransmit" commercial e-mail "with the intent to deceive or mislead recipients or [an ISP]" as to their origin.

- Falsifying the header information of the commercial e-mail you send.

- Setting up five or more e-mail accounts or two or more domain names with materially false identities and then sending commercial mail from any of the accounts or domain names.

- Falsely claiming ownership to five or more IP addresses, and then intentionally sending commercial e-mail from any such IP address.

Each of the crimes listed above kicks in at relatively low volumes, 101 or more messages within 24 hours, 1,001 or more messages within 30 days, or 10,001 or more messages within one year. Just think, send out 100 such messages in a day and you may face civil liability. Send one more and you may find yourself behind bars. Because no one yet knows how courts will interpret the law, you should not use those techniques.

2. Avoiding materially misleading header information
Falsifying header information is a crime. Misleading header information can result in a civil penalty. What's the difference between falsifying and misleading? It's hard to say at this time, but you should undertake the following steps to ensure squeaky-clean headers:

- If you send commercial e-mail from your own server, make sure the IP address listed in your e-mail header has a valid "Reverse DNS Lookup" associated with your domain name. You can check the reverse lookup of your IP address for free at www.dnsstuff.com.

- If you send commercial e-mail through an e-mail distribution service, place your company name and e-mail address in the "from" line. Most services offer this feature.

- Make sure that everyone in your company has their e-mail accounts properly configured in their e-mail client and their outgoing e-mail messages list their full name and e-mail address in the "from" line.

3. Using descriptive subject headings

The CAN-SPAM Act prohibits subject lines likely to mislead recipients about a "material fact regarding the contents or subject matter of the message." Even if you unknowingly mislead recipients, you may still be liable if under the circumstances a reasonable person would find the subject line materially misleading.

This requirement should not significantly impact legitimate businesses because it still allows for writing teasers and still allows for focusing on the content most likely to maximize the open rate. For example, every Tuesday www.marketingprofs.com distributes a newsletter that summarizes and links to the latest articles. Because of technical size limitations, www.marketingprofs.com could not possibly describe each article in the subject line. Fortunately, the law does not require a comprehensive description.

Notwithstanding this freedom, you should appoint someone to review and approve subject lines for at least your bulk distributions. In addition, testing subject lines will become more important than ever.

4. Allowing your reply address to function as an unsubscribe mechanism

Unsolicited commercial e-mail messages must feature either a return address through which someone can unsubscribe or another "Internet-based mechanism, clearly and conspicuously displayed." If used as an unsubscribe mechanism, a return address must remain functional for 30 days after a message is sent.

Until the courts or the FTC clarify what kind of unsubscribe links qualify as "clearly and conspicuously displayed," you should send e-mail from an address that someone at your company checks periodically (see below for specifics on frequency) for unsubscribe requests.

This way, if the tiny unsubscribe link at the bottom of your message is someday deemed noncompliant, your messages as a whole will still be compliant thanks to the reply address. For additional insurance, list the reply address somewhere in the message as well.

5. Handling all unsubscribe requests on at least a weekly basis

The CAN-SPAM Act mandates that companies refrain from sending unsolicited commercial e-mail to someone more than 10 days after that person submits an unsubscribe request.

This requirement does not necessarily mean that you must act on unsubscribe requests within 10 days. If, for example, you use your house list every four weeks, you have 28 days to act on unsubscribe requests. Nonetheless, you should consider handling such requests on at least a weekly basis for foolproof protection from violations.

If possible, you should also keep a record of each unsubscribe request and the action taken. Many e-mail distribution solutions can keep track of those who unsubscribe and the date they did so.

6. Centralizing Your Lead/Contact Database

Because the CAN-SPAM Act attributes e-mail messages sent by an individual to the entity promoted in the message (your company or one of its divisions), the time has come for companies to rethink the way they manage the e-mail addresses of prospects and customers.

If your company has several different lists, or if your salespeople have their own personal lists, you should centralize these disparate lists into one multi-user database.

The easiest way to accomplish this is by using an e-mail distribution service (e.g., ActionMessage, Cheetah). If your contact/lead management needs exceed the capabilities of such services, you should implement a customer relationship management system, whether software (e.g., GoldMine, Siebel) or an online service (e.g., Salesforce.com, SalesNet.com).

The bottom line is that when someone unsubscribes, you need to make sure that no one else in your division/company (depending on the circumstances) e-mails that person again.

7. Creating a standardized identifier for e-mail solicitations

Unsolicited commercial e-mail must provide "clear and conspicuous identification that the message is an advertisement or solicitation." The CAN-SPAM Act does not provide any specifics (except in the case of pornographic material) on how to comply with this requirement.

Although many companies will use the "ADV" abbreviation (short for advertisement) in the subject line (which rose to prominence thanks to various now-defunct state laws intent on curbing spam by at least warning the user they were receiving an advertisement), the CAN-SPAM Act does not require this approach. Because many spam filters look for "ADV," you should not use it.

A better solution is to create a standardized identifier for your company. For example, you might begin each subject line with your company's name or an abbreviation. Since there is no requirement that this identifier reside in the subject line, you could instead place something at the top of your messages.

Incidentally, if you have affirmative consent, you need not provide an identifier in your commercial e-mail messages. However, until the courts address the scope of affirmative consent, your best bet is to comply with this requirement.

8. Listing your company's street address

The CAN-SPAM Act requires the inclusion of "a valid physical postal address of the sender" in every unsolicited commercial message but does not indicate whether a post office box will suffice.

Until a definitive answer exists, you should use a street address. If your company does not have a street address or you do not want to list it because you work out of your home, you can rent a virtual street address for approximately $100–$200 a month from companies such as HQ Global Workplaces and Regus.

Since the law applies to even a lone commercial e-mail message, you should require all employees (or at least your salespeople) to place a company-approved signature containing your street address at the end of every e-mail message they send. Too few companies take advantage of the marketing potential of standardized signature lines. Therefore, this requirement may boost rather than reduce sales.

Third-party e-mail lists: the controversy and an alternative interpretation

The CAN-SPAM Act has implications for a common activity, third-party list rentals. A number of marketing professionals have interpreted the CAN-SPAM Act as requiring multi-company list cleansing even when affirmative consent exists. In other words, they claim that if you run a full-message e-mail ad (or "blast" as some refer to it) on a third-party list, and a recipient requests removal, both you and the third-party must remove that person from your respective lists.

This interpretation would set an impossible bar for many legitimate businesses, at least until they upgrade their e-mail marketing technologies or some neutral body establishes a centralized clearinghouse. It also likely violates countless privacy policies and fails to address many common scenarios.

For example, what if the recipient subscribes to your list in the process of responding to your ad, and then unsubscribes from the third-party list? To make matters worse, what if the recipient does not click the unsubscribe link in the ad until several months after distribution?

Fortunately, an interpretation exists that is more plausible, though not yet validated (so rely on it at your own risk), thanks to four key provisions:

- First, the unsubscribe provision of the CAN-SPAM Act applies only to "senders" and those who act on their behalf (i.e., the third-party list owner).

- Second, the law uses the term "initiate" to describe the act of sending commercial e-mail oneself or through a third party.

- Third, the law defines "senders" as those who *both* "initiate" *and* "whose product, service, or internet website is advertised or promoted by the message" (i.e., only you, *not* the third-party list owner).

- Fourth, the law circumscribes the extent to which commercial e-mail from a "sender" can be attributed. For example, if a message makes it clear that it comes from a "division" of a larger entity, then unsubscribe requests apply only to that division, not to the entire entity.

Apply this logic to third-party lists, and if the list owner frames (wraps) your ad within its own branded template, you can argue that any unsubscribe requests apply only to the list owner's lists and not your own. The list owner's branded template is key, because it essentially transforms the list owner into the "sender" or, alternatively, into a "division" of yours. Put differently, subscribers must feel that the ad has been sent by the list owner rather than by you.

With this interpretation, you need not unsubscribe anyone from any of your own lists. An argument can also be made that the list owner does not have to remove those who unsubscribe from all of its future mailings, but rather only future mailings on your behalf. However, for the time being, list owners should adopt a more conservative approach and never e-mail these people again unless they later rejoin the list.

As for you, the following guidelines will likely keep you out of trouble:

- Make sure that the list owner complies with the eight steps listed in the previous section. For good measure, make sure that you yourself comply with steps 3 (descriptive subject) and 8 (street address).
- Make sure that the list owner frames your ad within its own branded template that clearly indicates to recipients the origin of your ad and the extent to which unsubscribe requests will be attributed.
- If you run a subsequent ad on the same list more than 10 days after running the initial ad, verify that the list owner has removed previous recipients who requested removal.

A final word
Federal regulation is no picnic, but it need not stifle your e-mail marketing plans. However, you should implement a compliance program and appoint someone to be in charge of compliance with

CAN-SPAM regulations and to stay abreast of new developments, such as court opinions and FTC regulations.

A compliance program will not provide you with an absolute defense to a CAN-SPAM violation, but it will significantly lessen the likelihood of such a violation in the first place and, should such a violation occur, it could significantly mitigate damages.

10. Unsubscribe Link Spam Compliance

Common unsubscribe methods you can use.

Having a working unsubscribe mechanism in your e-mail is not only a key provision of CAN-SPAM, it's also always been a best practice in e-mail marketing. Are you taking full advantage of the opportunity? Some marketers view "unsubscribe" as their nemesis. But if you optimize the process, you not only make leaving easy for readers, you can gain valuable feedback and possibly get them to opt-in for different e-mail communications, or plant a seed for them to re-subscribe.

The four common unsubscribe mechanisms are:

- **Reply/remove:** Subscribers reply with "remove" or "unsubscribe" in the subject line.
- **General link:** Subscribers click to land on a page where they enter their e-mail addresses.
- **Customized link:** Subscribers click a link coded with your e-mail address and land on a page confirming the remove.
- **Subscription management system:** Subscribers click and land on a page with personal and e-mail subscription information, which can be modified.

Tips for Optimization

Unsubscribe mechanisms
I always recommend my clients incorporate at least two unsubscribe mechanisms into their e-mail. This gives some insurance should one not work (an even more important consideration now that CAN-SPAM rules the land). It also makes getting off your list easier. I further recommend one of the mechanisms be what I call "reply/remove."

You should all be familiar with reply/remove, so I won't say too much. It was one of the first unsubscribe mechanisms available. In the early years, we really trained people to do this to get off a list. For that reason, I want to ensure the method works.

Your IT group may try to talk you out of using this method. Don't let them. Some IT groups prefer to use a "do not reply" address for the send. This eliminates the need to sift through replies. (In addition to unsubscribe, you may get feedback you must read and perhaps reply to, not to mention out-of-office messages.) From a customer service perspective, it's better to keep this channel open for unsubscribes and other communications.

General/customized links
These are also pretty straightforward. I prefer customized links. It's one less step for the reader to take to be removed. One caveat: A custom link may allow the actual subscriber to be removed by someone the e-mail was forwarded to. I haven't seen this happen with any frequency, but you should be aware it's a possibility.

As insurance, always send an e-mail confirming the unsubscribe. That assures people aren't removed from your list without their knowledge. Another safeguard: Password-protect the system (and don't include the password in the e-mail) so only the actual subscriber can make changes.

Subscription management systems
Subscription management systems offer the best opportunity to make the unsubscribe work for you. They can also save administrative time and are a tremendous tool in complying with CAN-SPAM.

A subscription management system gives subscribers access to their account information. They're able to update personal information (e-mail address, name, etc.) and view/change subscription options. If you offer more than one e-mail newsletter or type of e-mail communication, you can list them all on the system. Subscribers can opt in or opt out at will.

Some marketers fear subscribers will opt out of everything. Smart marketers realize that giving subscribers options and allowing them to make their own choices about what they want to receive will result in a more engaged subscriber base. They may unsubscribe from newsletter A but opt in to receive newsletter B.

The other huge benefit is something subscribers don't see: the back end. That's where a list of unsubscribes is kept. You may need the list as a suppression file to comply with CAN-SPAM.

It's also where you'll have a record of all opt-ins, including date, time, and the IP address they came from, to use as proof of affirmative consent. Having a list that can be proven to be affirmative consent may get you out of some potential
CAN-SPAM requirements going forward, including the Scarlet Letter: adding "ADV" to the subject line and (already written into the law) a notice in the e-mail body that it's a commercial message.

Does subscription management sound expensive? It doesn't have to be. E-mail vendors at all price points include subscription management capabilities in their standard offerings.

Other Quick Optimization Tips

- **Tell them which e-mail address you're sending to.** Always include a note in the e-mail footer that lists the e-mail address you send to. This is especially important if the recipient's e-mail address doesn't appear in the recipient line (e.g., if you use the BCC line or a hidden address distribution list for the send). Many people use e-mail forwarding. If they try to use a reply/remove mechanism, it probably won't work. The e-mail it's sent from isn't the one in the list owner's database.

- **Include unsubscribe URLs.** Just in case links aren't live (a common feature in many new spam filters), include the actual URL of the unsubscribe or subscription management link in the e-mail body. If the link doesn't work, subscribers can still copy and paste the actual URL into their browsers and get to the subscription management system or off the list.

- **Unsubscribes don't just happen online.** CAN-SPAM requires you to have a process to fulfill unsubscribe requests within 10 days, no matter what channel they come through: online, USPS mail, telephone, and so on. Be sure people at each contact point know how to handle the requests.

- **Send an e-mail confirming the unsubscribe.** You should always send an e-mail confirming the unsubscribe. An auto-responder including the address removed and the date is the best way to go. You won't be in violation of CAN-SPAM in so doing. You have 10 days to remove them from your list; so one more e-mail within that period is covered.

The smartest organizations use this message as an opportunity. They gently invite readers to re-subscribe at any time, include a link to do so, and ask them to save the e-mail for their records. Even smarter: ask people to tell you why they're unsubscribing. Few will respond, but you may get some information you can use to improve the content, frequency, or focus of your e-mail messages. Often, you'll get assurances they aren't really leaving, just changing e-mail addresses or going on vacation.

Unsubscribe is for the long term
Keep a suppression list of your unsubscribes. According to CAN-SPAM, you cannot mail them again unless they provide affirmative consent, that is, opt back in to your list. This is especially important

if you rent third-party lists. You must suppress anyone who ever previously unsubscribed from your lists.

Some discussion with the Federal Trade Commission (FTC) suggests this could apply to one-on-one e-mail sent by your sales force. You may need to suppress these names from your sales force management system, too.

Thinking strategically about unsubscribe mechanisms can help keep your e-mail lists engaged, encourage growth, and keep you in line with CAN-SPAM regulations.

Checklists

Security

What spam filtering software are you using?

_____

What is the normal subject of your commercial message?

_____

Where is your message listed (websites that have your info)?

_____

Do you know who sends out messages with your name on it)?

_____

What permissions do you ask for before you send out an email to someone?

Single opt-in: _____

Confirmed opt-in: _____

None: _____

How do you remove email addressed from your list?

_____

_____

_____

_____

Outreach Checklist

What potential customers do you want in your outreach program?

Customer   Value to You (1 to 10)

1. _____   _____

2. _____   _____

3. _____   _____

4. _____   _____

5. _____   _____

List at least 3 industries you target for your Marketing campaigns_

Industries   Rank (1 to 10)

1. _____   _____

2. _____   _____

3. _____   _____

Which of these industries would work well using an email campaign?

_____

_____

List 5 freebies you could offer to rental list email recipients that would make them click on your link.

_____

_____

_____

_____

_____

Commercial Message:

Write a sample commercial message you would use and send to a rented list. Remember be creative but have a call to action.

_____

_____

_____

_____

_____

List 5 things you expect to include in your newsletter. How many of these are sales pitches rather than information?

_____

_____

_____

_____

_____

Name at least 8 things you can do to become CAN-SPAM compliant

_____

_____

_____

_____

_____

_____

What 2 mechanisms will you use if someone wants to unsubscribe from your email list?

_____

_____

NOTES

4. Know Your Segments

1.   *Auto Responders*

> Are you willing to let your competitors
> outmaneuver you ?

Auto responders are magic! More and more companies will embrace
the sizzle behind the auto responder's deliberate intent to further
activate the end user. Are you willing to let your competitors
outmaneuver you in this arena?

Look inside the arena and imagine all the assets you offer. Now
picture any segment of your customer or prospect base visiting your
website and requesting more information on any or all of your value
proposition.

The results you'll find in using auto responders can be amazing.
Strategize why you would want to send an auto responder after a
visitor completes or does not complete a transaction. Auto
responders are fabulous for making smaller companies look even
more connected to their e-mail recipients or website visitors. If an e-
mail recipient viewed the e-mail and didn't click to the landing page,
perhaps you follow up with an auto responder, offering an even
greater value to incite a response.

You might send an auto responder to a website visitor who did sign
up for your offer, then failed to act on the value of the offer. Send
them an e-mail that provokes action. The auto responder is truly one
of the most unused pieces of e-mail marketing and under
appreciated marketing deliverables of any I've seen. Get in the auto
responder game and win the internet marketing game.

Auto responders can be set up to shoot back an e-mail message
automatically depending on what type of goal you want to attain. A
great example is offering your web site visitors a seven day mini-
course that will send an e-mail once a day for one week. The magic is
in e-mail marketing working for you while you build your business in
many other ways.

2.   *Preference Centers*

> What drives a preference center is the desire to offer
> up a dialogue with your opt-in
> permission-based end user.

Best practice companies invite customers to opt in for specific kinds
of information. For example, a banking customer might want
mortgage information when interest rates dip below a specific

threshold or information about privacy protection and identity theft (and nothing else). Often this kind of collaboration on interests is supported with website personalization. If your company extends this courtesy on the website, leverage the insight into your customer for e-mail marketing campaigns.

Personalization can give the customer a lot of control over what appears in his or her mailbox and computer, as well as help the company assess interest in new products and services even before marketing offers are made.

What drives a preference center is the desire to offer up a dialogue with your opt-in permission-based end user. If retention of anyone in your database is of interest to you, consider a preference center to be where relationships blossom between you and your customer. This means that if you have the profile of your prospect or customer in your database, you're one step ahead of your competition.

Customers will graciously offer up numerous individual preferences special to them if you give them the chance. This is the perfect example of where preference centers can make an enormous difference in knowing more of what satisfies your recipient. Asking better questions of your website visitor can dramatically enhance the customer experience. Almost everyone in your permission-based database has opted in for e-mail messaging from you or your company. You better believe they will gladly let you know which of your products, solutions, or services are their favorite or they may want to decline receiving a particular piece of your content.

Philosphy.com is a cosmetic firm that has embraced the preference center concept, and they understand the value of asking questions that will help them segment their customers' preferences. The results are staggering in terms of Philosophy's increasing long-term revenues. When any company sends you an e-mail with content that you requested from the preference center, that company is trying to build loyalty with you and strengthen their brand equity with you as well.

A great example of relationship marketing through the preference center is the question, "Would you like gift giving suggestions via e-mail?" When a gift giving suggestion e-mail was deployed to the segment of the audience that had answered yes, the result was a huge increase in sales for Philosophy. This is relationship marketing at its finest and an e-mail campaign at its highest level of relevance.

Most often response rates soar, including opens, click-throughs, and conversions on the landing page—conversion being a website purchase by a Philosophy customer directly in response to the e-mail gift-giving suggestion. Philosophy also realized that many who had once offered their profile to the preference center were now requesting more, such as the monthly e-newsletter and enrollment in the birthday program.

The point is to gather customer interests on your website signup form and use them. It may be tempting to send an all-purpose e-mail to your entire audience regardless of their stated preferences, but established best practices and the DoubleClick study strongly indicate that, from the recipient's viewpoint (the only one that really matters), irrelevancy can easily turn a good permission-based e-mail into spam.

Take the time to learn more about content, relevance, and frequency by enabling your visitors, clients, customers, or members to choose what kind of information they want to receive from you. When someone signs up to be on your e-mail list, allow the person to select his or her areas of interest.

For example, allow subscribers to select by:
- Product or service categories.
- Job function or self-description.
- Desired communication type or content(e.g., newsletters, event or sale notifications, new product or service announcements).

Also, specify what the customer will receive and when; for example, "Sign up for our Hart Creative Marketing Quick Tip, sent every Friday, and become an expert e-mail marketer!"

Marketing should not be thought of as linear or one-dimensional. The goal is to find ways to lengthen or enrich the dialogue with current customers. Also, remember the importance of driving traffic to this section of your website, the birthing agent to a long-term relationship with your customers, prospects, and suspects (visitors suspected of being interested in buying your product or service)—any and all visitors to your site, including your most precious satisfied customers who hold your company near and dear.

Another interesting example of offering preferences comes from a hearing aid company whose customers had received a printed newsletter for many years. Wanting to cut its printing costs, the company offered their customers the choice of receiving an e-newsletter or a printed, mailed newsletter, or even both. The customers were notified of the offer by e-mail and made their choice by e-mail. How did the company capture their e-mail addresses? The company requests that all patients who visit the preference center give up their e-mail address for ongoing opt-in e-mail communications.

What a way to say "we respect you and your preferences." Giving the customer the choice to set a preference is just like a server in a restaurant not presuming you want your cocktail "on the rocks."

Wouldn't that be offensive? It's the same with e-mail marketing. The first e-newsletter sent to a new customer even clearly highlights how much the company appreciates the customer's business and solicits the customer's assurance of permission to further communicate in the inbox.

Be very careful when delivering an e-mail to your database for the first time. Instead of only requesting permission to send one type of e-mail, like an e-newsletter, also offer the opportunity to opt-in to additional offers, event announcements, educational highlights, notice of a company move to a new location, etc. I'll explain more about these preference options in a moment.

3. Segmentation

Have a better understanding of your customer.

Do you want a better understanding of your customers?

- Do you want to drive customers higher and higher up the value chain?

- If you knew them better, could you improve your communication with them?

- Would you like to know which customers are generating profits and which are eroding profits?

Segmenting Your Customers by Needs and Psychographics

Segment your target audience	Different audiences probably need to be approached differently. For example, different segments will be motivated by different tactics and messages. Here's an opportunity to develop verbiage and programs accordingly.
Prioritize target groups	Rank the segments in order of priority by size and potential profitability.
Leverage or develop value propositions for each audience	Using survey results and interviews with your sales team, have your marketing team look at how you target various client groups, and which current resonant messages can be utilized for business development.

Develop promotions and interactive web selling pages to appeal to each group	If you don't already have them, develop promotions to drive the behavior you want to encourage.
Value-based decisioning	Can you predict a customer's future value and base your business strategies around that value? Value-based decisioning assists in understanding and proactively managing the value of each customer. Here you have an important choice. You can take your chances and hope that a customer turns out profitable, or you can minimize your risk in the relationship and get as much information as possible to monitor, understand, predict, and therefore proactively manage customer value.
Monitor results from different sales channels, communications, and offers	A crystal ball sometimes seems to be the only way to predict your customers' behavior—particularly what types of products they will buy and how much and for how long, and ultimately how profitable they will be over time. Behavioral scoring helps remove the guesswork and provides valuable insight.
Benefits	All segment-based strategies need to be implemented in a test and learn framework where multiple experimental campaigns run simultaneously. The goal is to apply what is learned from those campaigns by improving future campaign offerings and by more sharply defining target segments. Over a period of time you should be able to increase value per customer and decrease expenses on spend enhancement campaigns.

Customer Survey	The best way to find out what motivates clients to buy from you is to ask them. Your goal is to uncover your unknown strengths, weaknesses, opportunities, and threats and then develop messages that will increase the effectiveness of sales and marketing efforts. We suggest surveying your client base to find out: Why they buy from you instead of or in addition to other firms How they want to be communicated with How they get information about your products Which product-related topics are of greatest interest or concern to them Deliverables would include: Survey strategy Question development Design of html and text e-mails to request survey participation Design of print direct mail piece to request survey participation Web page for online survey Copywriting for the deliverables listed above

Segmentation begins with your audience and your advertisers. Decide what to measure, how to measure it, and then start measuring. You record a mix of content interactions to establish the conventions of the customer behavior being measured and the minimum number of times a member visits before being assigned to a segment. We use a simple formula: tgp.emy18.com/
The frequency of an interaction over time equals a behavioral segment. The exact value for each variable may change depending on the segment being built, but the formula remains the same.

Deciding which interaction you want to track is simple enough, but the secret sauce is in how high a bar is set for segment membership. Make the frequency count too high and the segment is too small to matter. Define a lengthy time frame and the segment becomes homogenized, causing low response due to irrelevant ads being served.

When used as a framework for comparison, the elements of an effective behavioral targeting solution will help you set proper expectations and realize success. Behavioral targeting is all about delivering the right ad to the right person so he or she can buy something. With the right perspective, behavioral targeting won't get lost in the hype and will become a standard, and familiar, tool.

Naturally, the growth in targeting options makes media planning even more important. Media can now be purchased in almost any format imaginable (and combinations thereof): broadband/dial-up, look and feel of a message, past advertiser interactions, and publisher surfing profiles represent just a handful of online media options.

By utilizing effective segmentation schemes, you can generate significant improvements in performance. For three recent Hart Creative Marketing, Inc., campaigns, published research cited lifts in conversion rates ranging from 167% to over 3,100% for targeted media relative to untargeted advertising.

Anyone who is not experimenting with targeting runs the increasing risk of being outmaneuvered by clever competitors. At the same time, any company that focuses solely on media targeting without giving serious thought to the creative process is making an increasingly common and costly mistake.

Understand that once your campaigns have been delivered, rather than looking at overall response rates, you can determine the quality of the customers that the campaign acquired. Do they "look like" the company's most valuable customers? Are they "growable customers," that is, those customers capable of providing higher levels of response if the right offer is made?

By filtering metrics and campaign performance through this vantage point, you can ensure that the initiatives are attracting and retaining not just customers, but the right customers. Ultimately, segmentation will reap you more successful campaigns with higher returns.

4.   *Perfect Partners*

> Enhance their targeting efforts with relevant and innovative creative.

In the most successful online targeting campaigns, effective segmentation schemes go hand in hand with innovative creative.

As an example, consider the marketing challenge faced by a national broadband provider. A very simple targeting scheme would deliver different messages to dial-up users (much faster at a comparable cost), broadband surfers (switch now, first month free), current customers (free month for each referral) and lapsed customers (reduced monthly rate). Tailoring relevant messages to each specific segment would likely vastly enhance campaign performance.

Alternatively, consider a luxury automobile manufacturer that implements a simple re-messaging targeting scheme aimed at past site visitors. Recognizing that automobiles are a longer lead time, highly considered purchase, and well aware that past site visitors comprise some of the most highly qualified potential buyers, the manufacturer could afford to message this smaller, highly qualified audience with larger creative sizes and rich media. More expensive and compelling creative would reinforce key selling points and evoke strong emotion and aspiration among these past visitors.

While it sounds simple, incredibly, many online marketers fail to enhance their targeting efforts with relevant and innovative creative. As a result, these marketers may erroneously conclude that targeting does not work, when, in fact, the real problem lay with their irrelevant creative.

To maximize the effectiveness of targeted media, you're probably better off following several principles from the very start of campaign planning:

Start with a strong campaign brief
Prior to launching any targeting efforts, you should take the time to craft a thoughtful and detailed campaign brief. The brief should describe each potential customer segment and should require that both targeting scheme proposals and potential creative treatments fit against these segments.

Plan to test different messages to each unique segment
For each unique customer segment, several different creative themes and messages should be tested. Within two weeks after launch, the best treatments can be identified and further improved.

Be patient
Advertisers or marketers should not expect best results at launch. Rather, ongoing testing and optimization of media and creative combinations can achieve far stronger performance after four to six weeks.

5.   Email Campaign Management

> Strive to acknowledge the customer as an individual.

E-mail is a dazzling prospect for marketing because it offers precise timing and delivery of communication to customers. If those communications are relevant, personalized, and easy to understand, customers are more likely to respond favorably. When they do, customers expect a company to have fulfillment policies, procedures, and enabling technology comparable to, if not better than, those used to extend the offer. Delays at the back end ultimately undermine just-in-time communications at the front end.

Best practice companies strive to acknowledge the customer as an individual. Customers notice a misspelled name, particularly if they provided correction and the company failed to use it. A client of mine had an interesting experience relevant to personalized communication. A friend recommended a fabulous shampoo and conditioner sold by an online beauty retailer. The website was gorgeous and easy to navigate; it was simple to place and confirm an order. Imagine her surprise when she received a form e-mail letter several days later addressed to "Dear Customer" explaining that the item she ordered was out of stock.

They knew her name when she ordered and paid (it appeared in the confirmation), but the company did not know her when there was a problem. Her ordering experience was a dream, but the company's failure to link ordering with delivery and follow-up soured her on the purchase experience. (The firm subsequently succumbed to the dot com bubble burst.) The best marketing, sales, and purchasing experience can be completely undermined by conforming customer communications to a single, generic template.

6. *Effective Personalization Means . . .*

> Personalize the subject live with a concise offer statement that reflects an understanding of the customer's needs.

Use the customer's name in the "to" line of the e-mail offer as well as any follow-up communications.

Resist the temptation to pepper the offer with the customer's name. That just looks manipulative and manufactured; but make it clear that you know to whom you are extending the offer.

Identify the sender in the "from" line of the e-mail offer
Personalizing communication to the customer implies a quid pro quo. Plus, the call center may better support an offer by funneling all calls to the person identified in the "from" line. It is more personal and efficient!

Technology makes it easy to insert names into text, but use the capability sparingly. Personalize enough to make the customer feel recognized but not so much that the customer feels stalked or perceives the company as creepy.

In the 1990s, early adopters of call center systems that use Caller ID to retrieve customer records for the call center representative before connecting the two parties got a negative reaction from customers when the representatives answered inbound call using the customers' name: "Hello, Bob. How can I help you today?" Customers were made uncomfortable by this gesture and wanted to identify themselves. With campaigns, the message needs to be relevant but avoid personal details. You may know that the customer has an 18 year old leaving for college, making a "student bill presentment and payment" offer attractive. Use that information to craft the offer and target the customer, but avoid including that information to communicate the offer. Doing so may feel invasive to today's customer.

Personalize the subject line with a concise offer statement that reflects understanding of the customer's needs.

When the following subject line appeared in my mailbox from Amazon.com, I immediately clicked through and ordered: "Save 30% on David Sedaris Live at Carnegie Hall." Why? I had searched for the recording several months before, so the offer was relevant and I knew so by the subject line. (Note, the customer's name should not be part of the subject line—a practice that increasingly connotes spam.)

The more rigorously customers are segmented and targeted for an offer, the easier it is to develop a subject line statement that is relevant to the personal interests of customers within the segment. Campaigns that target several different segments may need different subject lines to align with the interests of each segment.

Some, but not all, best practice companies create different versions of offers to maximize appeal to different customer segments. Suppose, for example, the offer targets young singles. What if some of the singles are part of a couple? Would the singles message be relevant or a blunder? The issue here is to be sure that assumptions are challenged and the resulting offer is described in a way that is relevant. The same customer data used to target the customer is essential to optimizing the offer for relevance. Some innovative companies have customer advisory boards whose job is to measure and provide feedback on and validation of assumptions, messages, and marketing approaches and their effect on the customer experience. Maybe this approach is practical for your company.

7.   *Customer Acceptance is the Goal*

> Target only those customers who are likely to accept.

Customer acceptance is the goal of every campaign, whether the marketing organization subscribes to the mass market or one-to-one philosophy of marketing. Best practice companies design and execute e-mail campaigns that:

- Target only those customers who are likely to accept, that is, who want or need the offer at the time it is made. Correct timing is just as important as matching other aspects of the offer to the customer's preferences and behaviors.

- Budget the campaign in relation to its potential return. Knowing the value of the targeted customers and achieving a high acceptance rate helps assure an acceptable return on investment.

- Use information about the customer to decide whether or not he or she should be targeted for a given campaign. Behavioral information is more revealing and reliable than most demographic information, so pay attention to past purchases and their context.

- Measure and analyze the results of every campaign with the long-term goal of achieving 100% acceptance of any given offer because 100% of the target segment found the offer relevant and compelling.

Handling e-mail operations can be a tall order, but start with a good plan and build infrastructure over time as resource constraints allow. A good plan can overcome lack of technology, save time, and retain customers when the unexpected occurs:

- Make sure customer service is alerted to the campaign. Some customers will use other channels to respond or to ask for additional information about an e-mail campaign. The call center is particularly vulnerable, and needs time to prepare. In best practice companies, customer service is an acknowledged stakeholder and is involved in campaign planning. In addition, marketing provides support materials and may even do training sessions with customer service a week or so before campaign launch.

- Assign responsibility for monitoring and resolving incoming e-mail.

Providing unique inbound e-mail boxes to receive campaign responses can help get customer e-mail regarding the campaign into the right hands faster. However, be prepared for customers who read the campaign, then go to the website to respond, and therefore send the campaign-related mail to a different inbound mailbox. Similarly, customers may use the campaign mailbox to submit complaints, suggestions, or questions that have nothing to do with the campaign. If your company is concerned with maintaining and enhancing customer relationships, the system will resort to inbound mail to assure it gets to the person who can act on it.

For a variety of reasons, a portion of the e-mail campaign will "bounce," meaning the campaign will not reach the customer because the e-mail address is invalid, incorrect, or no longer exists. Monitoring bounced campaigns allows:

- Correction of erroneous addresses so that the offer can be reissued and the customer has an opportunity to respond. The customer who does not receive the campaign cannot accept the offer.

- Correction of the customer record so that future campaigns reach the customer, or at least prevent them from bouncing for the same reason. Bounced campaigns do not drive revenue.

- Identification of issues that may cause the e-mail host to refuse to send bulk e-mail. This is more likely to be a concern for companies that outsource the hosting of their e-mail services, but may be an issue if internal IT policies and procedures protect bandwidth. If no one knows the e-mail offers are not even making it out to the web, there will be no return on the marketing investment.

As a best practice, handling inbound mail is really part of back office readiness, but it warrants closer examination because companies consistently underestimate inbound volume. As a result, there is a substantial risk of customer dissatisfaction.

8.   Suspects

> Suspects are those who continuously subscribe to your e-newsletter.

Auto responders are magic! More and more companies will embrace the sizzle behind the auto responder's deliberate intent to further activate the end user. Are you willing to let your competitors In a mystery everyone who had "opportunity" is considered a "suspect." In an e-newsletter community of your customers and targeted prospects, every e-newsletter recipient is also seen as a "suspect." Unlike those at the crime scene, however, your mailing list members are not suspected of foul play. Your readers are suspected of being interested in buying your product or service. The mystery to solve is how to identify which ones are prospective buyers, so your sales team can spend their time wisely.

As in any good mystery, a suspect is one who just shows up. Suspects are those who continuously subscribe to your e-newsletter. These readers are not from a purchased mailing list. They are carefully chosen and connected to your organization. They appreciate your knowledge capital and will most likely hunger for more if you deliver the right message at the right time.

You will not please everyone all the time, so absorb it and accept it as the cost of doing business and the price we all pay for wanting to share the love, share the knowledge, and share how much you appreciate your community of permission-based e-mail recipients.

If a suspect unsubscribes from the e-newsletter, he or she is no longer visible to your organization. This lack of interest means one of two things: (1) Either the reader does not have a business problem that you can solve, or (2) the newsletter does not deliver good value (information) related to the business problem or the goods on offer.

In the first case, this is a good thing. No time or money needs to be spent on those who disqualify themselves. It's too expensive pursuing those who have little or no interest in the value you offer.

In the second case, you have a problem. You are losing suspects, not because they are no longer interested in the business problem you solve, but because the e-newsletter is not delivering high quality information about the business problem. Potentially valuable prospects may be unsubscribing from your newsletter due to poor content, not to a lack of interest in solving the business problem or purchasing your goods.

So how do you know whether or not you are delivering high quality information in your newsletter? This is where tracking comes into play. Many types of tracking technology are available that can be applied to your e-newsletter. These tools generate real-time feedback on unsubscribe rates, e-newsletter open rates, and article read rates.

With these statistics, you can see what articles your subscribers are reading, and just as importantly, what articles they are not reading. By focusing your content on popular topics, you will ensure both a high-quality newsletter and a high-quality prospect selection process whereby suspects unsubscribe to your newsletter only when they no longer have an interest in the good you offer or the business problem you solve.

9. *Filter Prospects From Suspects*

> Suspects come from a variety of backgrounds with many different needs and behaviors.

Start with this premise: All suspects are in complete control of their own buying cycle. They place themselves into your sales cycle in their time frame, not yours. The key is how to use the e-newsletter to identify when the suspect has turned into a prospective buyer.

Suspects come from a variety of backgrounds with many different needs and behaviors. As suspects become more and more interested in the services you have to offer, your relationship with them deepens and they become prospects. In e-newsletter marketing, every prospect comes from your suspect pool and can be filtered out by tracking their behaviors.

The following prospect levels show you how your relationship changes with the readers as they move themselves through your sales cycle from suspects to prospects to qualified leads:

Level 1: Suspect. Many of your e-mail recipients will eventually visit your website when you provide them easy links and ways back to the site from the e-newsletter. Suspects become prospects only when they click on a link that takes them to your website. This form of communication is one-way. They visit your site, but do not invite a two-way communication. Nevertheless, this is an indication they are interested in the information in the e-newsletter relevant to their everyday professional life, and interested in the company providing it.

Level 2: Prospect. Fewer readers go to the next level and begin two-way communication by filling out a reader survey about the e-mail message, or entering a contest to win a prize. This type of communication shows that they are not only interested in your company, but also willing to rely on your organization enough to interact more fully and submit information about themselves to you. These prospects are one step away from being a qualified lead.

Level 3: Qualified Lead. Prospects move to the final level, becoming a qualified lead, on their own accord, by responding to your "call to action," such as a free offer. They look to you when they interested a good you offer or need to solve a business problem that is addressed by the e-mail message and offered as a solution by your company.

Whether from the suspect pool or the prospect pool, this type of prospect becomes a qualified lead when he or she requests a free offer and fills out a questionnaire required to receive it. The prospect not only respects your e-newsletter information, but also believes in your company enough to provide you with the information needed to deliver a free service to him or her such as a ROI analysis or prototype marketing piece.

10. Prospects in the Sales Cycle

Why do prospects put themselves in the Sales Cycle?

Your e-mails or website presentation give your end users a means to trust that you are stable and understand their business. So when suspects arrive at your website from your e-mail and they receive your "call to action," they are far more likely to act on your call. Think of it in personal terms: Which stranger is more likely to accept your dinner invitation, someone who does not have a clue who you are, or someone who knows and respects your work?

This particular e-mail message is NOT a one-time direct mail piece. It is not a hard sell. The e-mail message is a patient conduit, attentive to your readers' natural buying cycles. I would place e-newsletters in this category as one of the most passive-aggressive ways of selling to your end user without appearing as if you were pushing for a sale.

Once you create an effective e-mail marketing process, you'll be amazed to see how quickly potential clients become interested in your services and identify themselves. Distributing your e-mail marketing consistently makes it easy for them to buy, rather than having your sales force try to sell them. This leaves one remaining piece of the puzzle: closing the sale. I can give you lots of technique and insight into closing the sale online coming in from any marketing channel. I can help you seed that incredible online relationship between a prospect and you.

What I can't do, nor would I want too, is give you the impression that there is some e-pill that you can swallow to magically hit the internet lottery. "Winning the internet marketing game," at the end of the day, entails a person who is willing to try out, through trial and error, how to give his or her customers the seamless buying experience of all time. No matter how we market with our dollars, the customer is just like you when you shop. The purchase occurs only when value equals perceived value of the sale minus the price paid. That will have you thinking for a moment I'm sure.

Checklists

List several places on you or any website where an autoresponder could be used..

_____

_____

_____

Name at least 5 preferences you can offer to your opt-in subscribers (that will enable you to send personalized information to them).

_____

_____

_____

List 5 discussion boards you can use to direct traffic to your website.

_____

_____

_____

_____

_____

_____

_____

List as many opt-in (aside from your newsletter) opportunities you can use to obtain permission for other types of email.

_____

_____

_____

_____

_____

List any item you will need to know about your customers in order to service them better.

_____

_____

_____

_____

_____

_____

_____

What will you use to measure the effectiveness of your email campaigns?

_____

_____

_____

_____

_____

List your customer segments (list as many as you can).

_____

_____

_____

_____

_____

_____

_____

What departments in your company are either directly or indirectly part of your email campaigns?

_____

_____

_____

_____

How do you plan to handle email orders?

_____

_____

_____

_____

What departments and who will be responsible for making sure products/services will be delivered on time?

_____

_____

_____

_____

List at least 5 popular topics in your industry.

_____

_____

_____

_____

_____

NOTES

5. Business Email & Web Strategies, Part I

1. *More Accountable to the Bottom Line*

Companies must justify budget allocations.

Companies must justify budget allocations and IT investments with results-driven business cases and prove value by showing bottom-line impact. There are two reasons for this.

First, technology has elevated the science of marketing, replacing vague decision making with fact-based analysis. Analytics, optimization, personalization, and event-based tools provide clear visibility into campaign performance. Comprehensive reporting provides insight on how to shorten marketing cycle times, lower production costs, avoid unprofitable campaigns, secure more qualified leads, and tweak campaigns in real time to boost results.

Second, the bottom-line pressure on companies will increase as more companies look to grow profitable customer relationships. The road to maximizing ROI and growing the value of the customer base begins here: Marketing is the critical front line where existing customers are retained and new ones are acquired. It is also the heart of customer intelligence, responsible for driving that insight across the business cycle through to sales, fulfillment, and service.

The world has plenty of technology with which to integrate and support your dreams and desires to increase your sales with less effort. Don't get caught up in the technology confusion or believe that you're not smart, curious, or patient enough to enjoy the benefits of building a community of e-mail addresses (a house list) and loyal fans along with elevating your website to a level that gains the respect of your customers and visitors.

When you have a plan building from the baseline of your current profits and losses, generating your offers to give the audience, creating compelling copy, double and triple checking for quality assurance, and measuring every angle you can, then you can count on attaining incremental gains. And more so, gain the most profit from the clients who appreciate you the most.

2. eMarketing Self Service

Do you want to take your online communications from average to spectacular?

Do you want to send a great professional-looking online newsletter to your clients and prospects? You don't have to go to expensive advertising or web development agencies. You can do it yourself. All you need is good to intermediate computer skills and the desire to learn what will best fit you.

Before I go any further I must make it clear that I'm a big believer in turning over the job to the craftsperson who delivers quality that comes from skill and experience. That can be hard for an entrepreneur to do, as most self-employed mavericks tend to not want to let go of their title as (pseudo) "marketing director."

Today the costs of e-mail marketing have fallen precipitously, making it more attractive to outsource your e-mailing marketing needs to a "new media" agency. New media is a term you will find when approaching agencies nationwide; it simply means digital media, and you will often find that description of agencies in any business directory.

Yes, some outsourcing to an agency might be necessary to get the expertise needed to integrate more than one e mail a month to one segment of an audience. Back when I had trouble affording marketing for my firm, self-serve was the only choice. But if I were searching today, and I wanted to still self-serve my e-mail marketing, I would definitely outsource. With e-mail marketing rates where they are today, almost all businesses can finally consider this a viable channel for spending their marketing budget.

Before I go into great detail on why self-serve e-mail deployment may work better for you than outsourcing, and before you spend countless hours ramping up the learning curve of e-mail marketing and the horrible return on time it can be in the first three months, allow me to share a word with you. The word is "leverage": Leverage the experts in the e-mail marketing arena to assist you and be amazed at what you gain.

Top three reasons? (1) Effective web, (2) e-mail presentation skills, and (3) quality assurance that each e-mail is delivered accurately and on time. If you are comfortable with poor return on time during the first three to six months of learning all the tips and tricks to sending the right message to the right person at the right time, then go self-serve.

For those who choose full-serve e-mail marketers or agencies to secure their e-mail campaigns and count on the results they expect to achieve, well, they also have disadvantages just as self-serve does. And some feel that investing ten to twenty hours a month learning a new tool to send e-communications to a permission-based e-mail list is worth all the effort.

3.   *Looking for an Email Service Provider*

What to look for in an email service provider.

I recently saw an ad for a self-serve e-mail marketing solution that went something like this:

Q. Can anyone tell me what I get for e-mail campaign setup fees?
A. We couldn't begin to tell you because we don't charge any.

The underlying message of the ad is that all campaign setup fees are a waste of money. But this is just not true. Many organizations struggle with time and resource issues, and others just want to ensure that their campaigns are professionally executed from day one. Having said that, it's important to ensure that you get your money's worth when hiring an e-mail services provider (ESP).

Quality Control of List
- **Unsubscribes**. If you submit a list for use in the mailing, your ESP should run that list against the unsubscribe file. Apart from being a good business practice, it's important in terms of CAN-SPAM compliance.

- **Soft bounces**. Similarly, your ESP should ensure that you don't attempt to send mail to addresses for which you've received a number of soft bounces. Soft bounces occur for a number of reasons. Some of the most common are: The domain exists but the e-mail address is invalid, the mailbox is full, or the receiving server was down or busy. A high bounce rate often indicates a list in need of maintenance. Also, and perhaps more importantly, if major ISPs and web-based e-mail services see that you're repeatedly attempting to send e-mail to bad addresses, you might end up getting blacklisted altogether.

- **Seed list**. This is easy to overlook. But the ESP should ask if there are any people at your company (who might not already be on the list) who need to see the campaign when it goes "live." The ESP should then add these e-mail addresses to the seed list.

Quality Control of Outbound Content

- **Review grammar and spelling**. Even if your ESP does not generate your content, a second set of eyes is always nice. Your service provider should be genuinely concerned with helping you put your best foot forward.

- **Review content for filters**, CAN-SPAM. Your ESP should run your creative files through a content checker to ensure that they are unlikely to trip common spam filters. When problems arise, suggestions for copy changes should be offered. Also, a quick review ensuring that you have a functional unsubscribe option and a complete snail-mail address should be part of this process.

- **Weight, size, and other specs**. Among other things, your ESP should ensure that your HTML file does not "weigh" more than about 25K to 30K, and that the file is not wider than practical, usually about 600 pixels. In addition, the HTML file should be a combination of images and text as opposed to one giant image (which, incredibly, I have often seen used).

- **Image weight and location**. Your service provider should either host images for you or ensure that your images are hosted correctly on your server (and that the HTML code is accurate). In addition, the ESP should check to see whether the images have been optimized for fast loading.

- **Text version**. Despite the availability of tools that claim to automate this process, you or your ESP should manually prepare the text version of your message. There should be no more than 60 to 65 fixed-width characters on each line, followed by a hard return. There should also be a decent amount of white space to optimize readability, and all hyperlinks should exist on unique lines with hard returns before and after the links.

- **Creation, hosting of web version**. Your ESP should generate a web-based version of your e-mail communication, and include a link to that version in both the HTML and text versions. Either you or your service provider can host this version, whichever is easier for you.

- **Link tracking and testing**. In addition to setting up link tracking, your ESP should assign "friendly" names to each link so that reporting will be easier to interpret. Also, each link should be checked prior to testing to ensure that it is functional and that the target is correct.

- **Internal test**. E-mail marketers' concerns with deliverability, filters, and spam issues make the internal testing process more important than ever. Your ESP should have a protocol established to send tests to major ISPs and web-based e-mail services to ensure not only that the mail is delivered but also that it is not routed to a junk-mail folder. Your ESP should also include test e-mail addresses using different software (such as Eudora, Lotus Notes, Outlook, and Outlook Express) to ensure that the message renders correctly and is not routed to a spam folder.

External test. The time that your ESP actually deploys your message should not be the first time that you see it "live." Rather, there should be an external test cycle with appropriate seed names from your organization so that approval can be given to deploy the mailing as instructed.

4.   Still Confused? Help is on the Way

Can the right vendor optimize your e-mail marketing?

Can the right vendor optimize your e-mail marketing? Maybe and maybe not. But the wrong one can definitely wreak havoc with results. Some marketers are unhappy with their current provider. Others are looking to enter the arena for the first time. I'm in the process of helping two clients choose a vendor. One client has an established e-mail program and is in need of a high-end solution. The other is new to e-mail marketing and looking for a low-cost provider. Here's the initial process I went through with both of them, one I've used many times over the years. You can easily commandeer this same approach to choose a broadcast e-mail solution for your organization.

Outsource Versus In-House Solutions
Many in-house IT departments are enthusiastic about managing a broadcast e-mail solution. Be careful. I've worked with IT departments that had the best intentions but quickly found themselves in over their heads. There was one group that mistakenly sent the first e-mail in "discussion list" mode, so everyone who replied to unsubscribe unwittingly sent their e-mail to the entire list. It was an honest mistake, but it hurt the company's standing with the people on their house list.
Outsourcing provides three key advantages:

- **Dedicated staff**. The outside vendors' job is to know e-mail inside and out, from technical aspects to ISP relationships to standards and best practices.

- **Adequate bandwidth**. The more e-mail you can send per minute, the quicker the message gets out. Outside vendors can do this without slowing down your internal systems or forcing you to send in the early hours of the morning.

- **Ongoing upgrades**. Competition forces vendors to keep their knowledge and systems up to date. Because of the time and cost involved, that's harder to do with an in-house system.

Many companies cite cost as a reason to bring e-mail in-house. Today, good outsource solutions are available at all price points, making cost a less-compelling argument. Unless you have a very strong technical team willing to dedicate people, systems, and other resources to e-mail, you're likely better off looking at outside solutions.

Estimate Your Usage
The most important aspects of usage are list size and send frequency. After determining these, you'll want to factor in any list segmentation or message versioning, auto responders, and viral marketing e-mail. I like to do a breakdown by month as well as an annual total. Most vendors have some kind of variable pricing based on the total quantity sent per month or year, as well as the number of versions. This information allows them to give you a price quote. It also helps you to estimate total annual cost.

Identify Your Needs
You're going to want the basics: tracking and reporting, list hygiene, some type of automated subscription/registration, HTML integrity check, a pre-send spam score, and so on. But don't stop there. Polls, surveys, online coupons, and other features can add real value to e-mail campaigns, depending on your industry and goals. Many vendors provide these capabilities as add-ons.

Determine Your Budget
As I mentioned earlier, there are great solutions at all price points, starting at $25 per month up to $15,000 per month and more. Do you get more with a more expensive solution? Yes, but many companies make out very well with more affordable packages that run $300–$5,000 per year. You'll sacrifice some support and ISP relationships, but you'll get the tracking and reporting, list hygiene, and basic functionality necessary to be successful. You can always trade up when you've got your e-mail marketing working so well you can justify a budget increase.

Narrow the Field
Many vendors can meet your needs and budget; you just need to identify them. I use a variety of methods to narrow the field, including:

- **Colleague recommendations**. Who do you know who's doing e-mail marketing? What are they using? How do they like their solution?

- **Case studies**. Often, articles or case studies reference vendors. Make a list and check them out. If a solution gets recognition for current clients, it could work for you as well.

- **Customer lists**. For a large client, I investigated which vendors worked with other companies in the client's general industry. Though we didn't want to go with a competitor's vendor, we knew that a company that served clients in our business area would be familiar with our needs and probably be able to meet them.

Learn as much as you can about each vendor from its website and from what comes back when you run a search on its name. Make notes and narrow the choices to those that not only meet your needs and budget but also make you feel most comfortable. Identify at least three, and no more than seven, vendors to look at in more detail.

Talk to the Vendors
For lower-end solutions, this may actually entail sending e-mail, although you can call many and speak with a representative. Smaller operations don't have outside sales reps. Your best bet is to research and do an overview of each, including a cost estimate. If you're looking at higher-end solutions, I strongly recommend writing a RFP (request for proposal). Use open-ended questions. Instead of asking if they track deliverability (where "yes" or "no" suffices as an answer), ask how they do it. I like to call and speak with representatives before I send an RFP. It increases the response rate. I also like to be available to answer any questions representatives may have. This allows them to target their responses and tells me how much they know about e-mail. Asking good questions during the due-diligence phase suggests they'll be on top of the account once my client becomes a customer.

Years ago I made a mistake that you should avoid: I talked to vendors who were not on my original list. They were friends of colleagues or people who had heard about the RFP and wanted in. With two of these, I spent a lot of time going through the RFP, explaining in detail what we needed to do and the functionality we required (something the vendors I'd chosen didn't need—they already knew). In the end, these "extra" vendors turned in proposals that were two and three times the cost of the other participants'. Basically, we'd pay for them to develop the capabilities we needed from scratch. It was a waste of my time and, to be honest, a waste of theirs.

5.   *Request for Proposal for Success*

**Why do prospects put themselves
in the Sales Cycle?**

In addition to being curious about whom we chose (and whom we didn't choose), people wanted a copy of our request for proposal (RFP), to help guide their own vendor searches. Naturally, I thought, "What better topic for my next column?" So here it is: a description of the RFP that got the job done.

RFP Format
Like any resourceful, efficiency-minded employee, not having written an RFP before, I took someone else's RFP and modified it. I stuck with the "outline" format of the original document, ending up with an RFP about 10 pages long, with the following main sections:
- Purpose
- Overview
- RFP Response
- Business Requirements
- Technical Requirements
- Support Requirements
- Pricing and Costs
- Summary

I solicited lots of advice. Why reinvent the wheel? The best advice I got was, instead of specifying what you need, let vendors tell you what their capabilities are. You do this by phrasing requirements as open-ended questions whenever possible. For example, instead of stating you need a maximum throughput of x million e-mails per month, you ask the vendor what their maximum e-mail throughput is. If you state, "I need x million," just about everyone will reply, "Yeah, we can do that." If instead you ask, "What's your maximum e-mail throughput?" you're likely to get a more thoughtful answer.

Introductory Sections
The first two sections of your RFP, Purpose and Overview, should be brief. The Purpose section is pretty straightforward: it's a short description of the purpose of your RFP. You are requesting a proposal from multiple vendors for a possible service relationship. The Overview section briefly describes your company and how you currently handle the function you need to outsource (e.g., Do you have an existing e-mail host?).

The third section, RFP Response, should be more substantial. We ask that responses take the format of the RFP itself: an outline that answers every bullet (item for item). You should request that the response address the vendor's product history, their implementation plan, process for customizations, training, and, of course, supply customer references.

Business Requirements

Now we're into the meat of the document. As this is an RFP for an e-mail delivery product, we asked vendors to provide information about their campaign management process. How do you choose a list? How do you filter out demographics, eliminate duplicate results, enter creative, send mailings? How do you get reports? What types of reports are available? Detailing these bullet points took up about a page and a half of the final document.

Consider the individual steps you take to get a mailing out. The vendor must address them all. At its simplest, first, you choose whom to send a message to. Second, you create your message. Third, you send it. Finally, you want reports on it. Your process is probably more complex than that.

Technical and Functional Requirements

The fifth section is perhaps the longest. In our final RFP it ran about three pages. This is where advice I received about asking open-ended questions really came in handy.

For technical requirements, we wanted to know what volume vendors could handle: maximum number of lists, maximum list size, maximum number of demographic details, and maximum number of e-mail messages sent per day. We also asked them to provide details on their profiling and demographic capabilities, any programmatic API interface to their system (so our developers could write scripts to automate campaign management if desired), what e-mail formats they supported (HTML, multi-part, etc.), what types of tracking they could do (open, click, etc.), and how the system handled e-mail distribution.

For functional requirements, we requested details on how vendors handled subscription management, customer service, abuse complaint resolution, and the other daily e-mail operations functions our team would need to handle. What are the functions you need to accomplish to get your mailings out, to add and remove people from your lists, and to deal with complaints? The vendor should make you feel comfortable on all of these points by addressing each of them.

Support Requirements

This section was pretty straightforward. What type of support do they provide via e-mail, telephone, etc.? Are there 24/7 beepers you can call? What's the guaranteed minimum response time?

Pricing, Cost, and Deadline

Again, pretty straightforward. First, what format does the vendor use to price their system? CPM (cost per thousand names), flat fee? Second, the question we've all been waiting for—what's their bid? Also, are there startup costs, additional support costs, costs for customizations, or other "hidden" costs? And of course at the very end, we provided vendors with a deadline for their proposals, and an e-mail address to submit them to.

6.   *Three Types of Email You Can Send*

What type of email is best for all my contacts?

Now that you have been enlightened on how to choose an e-mail provider, let's be sure you understand the three types of e-mail you can send:

- Plain text
- Simple HTML or rich text with simple formatting
- Advanced HTML with complex formatting, complete with tables, forms, graphics, and columns

Plain text
Plain text is just that. Very, very plain text. This is the only way to be technically sure that every single e-mail will be legible to the reader. You must have a plain text option for your online newsletter templates.

Defining HTML
HTML stands for Hypertext Markup Language. It's simply formatting instructions put in markers, called tags. Don't be afraid. The HTML coding is simply the e-mail (or web page) talking to your computer saying "make this text blue, end the paragraph here, put a graphic from this server right here, make this text bold and right align it." When you understand the concept, it really is quite simple.

Simple HTML
Your e-mail can have simple formatting text with it. You'll be able to change your font, its size, color, or alignment on the page (left, center, and right), and you can have bullet points or numbered lists. Your Outlook/Outlook Express e-mail formatting toolbar will show you exactly what you can do. Do not paste tables, columns, graphics, forms, etc., into Outlook, Lotus. You'll never know if the recipients see them in the form you send.

Advanced HTML
You know those e-mails you get that look like website pages? They're colorful. They have images. They could have built-in forms that you answer. Text can be arrayed in columns. There's background color. This is what is called advanced HTML. It's the next step up, and is simple to do once you know the basics and the tricks. But creating these e-mail and online newsletter templates does require the use of web designing software.

7. *Options for Personalized Email Merge*

Which option for email is best for my business?

Sending plain text or simply formatted e-mails

This first option is truly self-serve. In the mid '90s this was the only option for most professionals wanting to send e-mail to a bulk list of e-mail recipients. If your list isn't too big (above 50 to 100 e-mail addresses), why not use the Microsoft Office e-mail merge facility?

If you have Microsoft Office 2000 or a newer version, you can do a personalized e-mail merge or newsletter template (remember, simple formatting only) using Word as the base for the e-mail message. It then will link up to a database and create individual, personalized (with any field in your database) e-mails. The e-mails are routed to Outlook/Outlook Express and sent from there. MS Office 2000 can only do a plain text e-mail merge.

MS Office XP and 2003 do a beautiful, simple HTML e-mail merge. Remember, you can only use formatted text, bullet points, numbered lists. You cannot use graphics, tables, columns, pictures, or forms. Your help menu will assist you greatly through this process.

For e-mails with tables, graphics, or forms you need to go the next step up.

First, you must start working with advanced software, normally Microsoft FrontPage and Macromedia Dreamweaver. They are WYSIWYG (what you see is what you get) design tools that create the HTML code for you automatically.

You do have to become familiar with HTML coding. You don't need to know how to write code—the software does it for you—but you do need a basic understanding to fix problems if they occur.

If you want my candid opinion on self-serve e-mail delivery, leave it to experts. E-mail marketing is a tricky and sometimes wicked environment. You will not regret spending a bit more cash to have a great deal more time and much more peace of mind.

Finally, you may either outsource to a third party e-mail delivery service www.hartcreativemarkting.com (highly recommended) or an ASP, application service provider.

This is an online distribution service that will either give you access to their site to send your e-mails out over the internet, or they'll do everything for you. Or you can send them outbound yourself through your own ISP (which is not recommended).

8.   *Triggers*

What is a trigger when you are using email?

The future promises a larger shift toward integration of online, offline, and e-mail campaigns in customer acquisition and CRM (customer relationship management tools). Already web actions "trigger" online actions like e-mail and more targeted ad serving with advances in behavioral targeting. What we expect to see is more triggering between interactive actions like e-mail and form conversion online and non-traditional responses such as telemarketing and direct mail.

For example, when a consumer signs up at an automotive site for a new car quote, the following "triggers" can be set into motion:

- An auto finance offer is delivered through an exit pop-up.

- An auto-responder e-mail is sent containing an auto warranty offer.

- A car dealer who receives the consumer's request for a new car quote calls the phone number the consumer provided.

- That same car dealer sends the consumer a piece of direct mail containing more info on the dealership as well as additional partner offers from auto parts and services companies.

- Follow-up CRM e-mails, phone calls, and direct mail pieces may be sent over the course of time to retain, up-sell, and cross-sell that particular consumer.

There are many ways of integrating triggers into your existing business module, be it sending triggered messages such as order and service confirmations, billing, payment notifications, alerts, or information request responses (to name a few) to your customers based on certain criteria or account status. Effective use of your e-mail marketing tool and the incorporation of triggered messaging centralizes your customer communication. This also assists in generating productive reporting systems in order to monitor how specific campaigns are performing, which will in turn aid you in improving your marketing strategy.

As you set up triggered messaging to enhance your customer services, remember that the design of e-mail messages automatically deployed to customers must not only be meaningful and relevant but must also adhere to all CAN-SPAM rules. Subject lines must be carefully created to be catchy without being mistaken for spam or junk e-mail.

Automated correspondence to your customers with relevant information, depending on their account activity, will also promote excellent client services and improve website frequency rates as a result of repeat visits.

Triggered messaging should be seen as an essential tool when developing sound marketing strategies that will ultimately result in improved CRM and ROI figures.

9. RSS: Who, What, Where, When, Why

> Why do prospects put themselves
> in the Sales Cycle?

What are RSS Feeds?
RSS (Really Simple Syndication) pulls fresh content automatically from your favorite websites. It allows you to receive on your desktop an advisory with the date, a headline, a summary, and a link for each new item. If you want to read the full text, just click on the link.

More and more people will become more attached to RSS feeds where anyone who wants content from you can get it. You have probably noticed RSS invitations on websites. Those companies that do not provide a high volume of updated content do not have substantial incentives to participate in RSS feeds. A newspaper online is a great example of a website that would thrive with an RSS feed. Here is a sample of what you may decide to post on your website to give RSS availability to your website visitor.

- Hart Creative Marketing, Inc. News Delivered to Your Desktop

- Get the latest Hart Creative Marketing, Inc. marketing and product news delivered to your desktop. Our popular Quick Tip Emailer will provide you with up to the minute marketing techniques and keep you informed with our e-mail marketing legislation watch.

Get Started
Download and install an RSS reader on your computer. Dozens of newsreaders are available on the web, and most are free. Some of the more popular readers can be found by visiting the download.com site. Choose a reader that works best for your computer. We also recommend Pluck for your RSS reader.

- An alternative to downloading a dedicated newsreader is to use a web-based newsreader. For example, My Yahoo! users can now add RSS feeds directly to their personal page.

10.   How to Buy RSS Advertising

Setting the stage for buying RSS advertising.

RSS feeds are quickly becoming mainstream, but publishers, advertisers and consumers are just scratching the surface. Recent data from the Pew Internet Research Foundation shows that a mere 9% of the Internet population has a good idea of what RSS is. Don't be concerned about the numbers quite yet.

RSS is the new e-mail newsletter

RSS is poised to become an important content delivery mechanism in mainstream media. It will soon represent a permanent and fundamental change in the way information will be shared, viewed, and acted upon online. It will reshape the way people interact with the web for several reasons.

- E-mail spam has devastated the sending of legitimate customer communication—RSS is "spam free"
- Many publishers catering to the early adopter and tech markets are seeing 40% month-over-month growth rate in their RSS traffic. Some are seeing 50% of their traffic come from their RSS feed, with a corresponding decline in e-mail subscriptions
- RSS is easy to use (after the subscription process). Consumers will gravitate to anything that saves them time

RSS was popularized by blogs

RSS has been around for awhile, but not until very recently has there been a surge in its use. Why now? I believe there are two reasons.

- Explosion of blogs
- Demand for consumer control

Technorati reports over 900,000 blog posts are created daily. Blog software tools make publishing to the web as simple as typing an e-mail. RSS makes it easy to stay up-to-date with the volume of blog posts. The content comes to you. You no longer have to search for it.

A common misperception is you must have a blog to have an RSS feed. This is not so. RSS has been adopted by major publishers such as CNET, the BBC, Yahoo, Motley Fool, InfoWorld, The New York Times, the Christian Science Monitor, Wired News, The Wall Street Journal and many others, including a rapidly growing contingent of local and regional newspapers.

Era of consumer control

From TV and digital video recorders to radio and podcasts, consumers are demanding control over their media consumption. For over 50 years, TV and radio have remained the same. With the advent and popularity of TiVo and Podcasting, both TV and radio will see dramatic changes in how people interact with and consume these media. Consumers will watch and listen on their time, skip commercials, and create their own personal information gathering networks.

Because of RSS, online content consumption is changing too. You can now get your favorite content delivered right to your desktop and read it on your time—without the threat of spam clogging your inbox.

RSS is in its infancy

However, RSS is not perfect. It has a lot of growing up to do. Here are just a few things that will need to change before we see widespread adoption of RSS:

- Subscribing to feeds is cumbersome. It is not intuitive.
- Receiving feeds requires another tool (news aggregator) to adopt.
- Getting subscriber counts and data requires new enterprise software to employ.

I compare the sophistication of RSS today to the first banner ad that ran in 1994. Look where we are today with banners—animation, Flash, behavioral targeting, Fatboy Ad, affiliate programs, etc.

In the future, RSS will carry more than text. Today, it is already the primary distribution channel for podcasts. In the near future, much of the content delivered in the era of the much touted Web 2.0 will come on the backs of RSS feeds.

11. Add RSS to Your Marketing Mix

Why do prospects put themselves
in the Sales Cycle?

Only 5 to 10% of Internet users have actually tried RSS. So why is RSS getting such high visibility? One reason is that early adopters are a demographically desirable, technically savvy, information-centric audience. More important, RSS allows you to promote through a consumer-initiated content feed users sign up for and, hence, actually want.

RSS can be a useful addition to a marketing arsenal in several ways:

- **Drive traffic to your content**. For media entities, this can be important if content lives behind a firewall and isn't caught by search engines. Be sure to promote your top stories on the relevant pages to encourage further reading, as visitors don't enter your site through the home page.

- **Increase e-commerce**. Target product information feeds to meet customer needs and interests. As with e-mail marketing, where product is pushed to customers, ensure that presentation, promotions, and timing are relevant. Leverage existing offerings on your site and you may not need additional creative development. A regular content schedule is important. To keep RSS users and attract new ones, develop special RSS-only promotions.

- **Extend advertising and branding**. Perusing your headlines on a regular basis help keep your brand at the top of readers' minds. Further, branding can be incorporated in the way feeds are written. From an ad perspective, you can wrap branding into an RSS reader or buy advertising on RSS feeds using a service such as Pheedo. If your advertising, whether video, audio, or static, is engaging, consider using links to encourage users to view and interact with it.

- **Distribute corporate communications**, press releases, and investor relations content. Keep a broader constituent base informed. When disseminating corporate information via RSS, bear in mind the user decided to get your content, and your feed is public information. Make feeds short and informative to ensure recipients read them. Remember, you may not have control over the information environment in which your content is consumed.

Given current limited RSS use numbers, marketers must encourage RSS use. Among today's leading consumer offerings are Bloglines, NewsGator, and Pluck. This is a marketing issue because without an RSS-enabled customer base, program reach will be limited.

Help the process by developing promotions that entice customers to use RSS. Not all prospects are technically savvy, so consider how to convince users they'll benefit from subscribing to your content. Offer them free unique content or special promotions to make it worth their while. Also, promote RSS feeds throughout your site.

RSS gets around overstuffed e-mail inboxes and dreaded junk folders and gives anonymity to registrants, who may be concerned about sharing personal information. But it's not a substitute for e-mail marketing. Rather, it's another conduit for reaching your target market.

From a marketing perspective, RSS measurability is evolving but still limited. You can't tell who has received your feeds as you can with e-mail. Your company information may be interspersed with that of your competitors. In the current information environment, you can't tell how users gather information. So it's important to be part of the offering to have a chance of being heard. Some RSS readers, such as NewsGator, allow users to set up persistent searches to continually monitor important key words, such as your company name or brand. RSS results can be analyzed as follows:

- **Track new feed subscribers**. From a traffic perspective, though repeat visits are important, you must continually expand your reader base, especially to yield optimal results to your advertisers. Watch cancellation rates as well.

- **Monitor click-throughs from feeds**. Though you can't track specific customers, you can tell which content or product offerings drive usage. Also, measure time spent on site from RSS feeds. Among the factors to assess are when people view versus clicking—to determine what time of day to publish, what type of content to publish, and how many pieces to publish at a time. For e-commerce sites, track purchases and related metrics. Consider how to engage these customers and extend your relationship with them once they reach your site.

- **Measure RSS ad response**. Use impressions, CTR (click-through rate), actions, and costs (including CPM [cost per thousand names] and CPA [cost per acquisition]) to determine ad effectiveness. It should also help you determine the optimal mix of editorial content and advertising.

- **Assess costs**. Often, all that's needed is titling and encoding URLs, not creating special HTML or landing pages. This means the cost of initiating an RSS program with existing content is relatively limited. It's more a matter of how your company decides to make its content public. Given that RSS is an additional way to reach customers, you should consider testing the cost efficiency of different ways to get customers to subscribe to your feeds.

To get consumers to keep using your RSS feeds, you must continually supply new content that readers must find valuable. Though RSS currently reaches a relatively small user base, it's growing fast. Even today, it can be an important addition to your marketing mix, as it reaches consumers who might not otherwise engage with your content. In today's wired world, every company with a robust website is a content provider. Start thinking about and testing how to make RSS work for you.

Checklists

Where do you current obtain most of your profits (losses)?

_____

_____

_____

What do you expect to gain from an online campaign?

_____

_____

_____

How do you plan to use your website do generate profits?

_____

_____

_____

List 5 things you would like to accomplish with an email campaign.

_____

_____

_____

_____

_____

How large is your current email list?

_____

How often do you plan to send out information?

_____

_____

What type of email format will you use for your email campaigns? (HTML, RTF, Plain text, Advanced HTML)

_____

When a customer places an order on your website, what triggers could you put in place to up and cross-sell?

_____

_____

Name 3 things where RSS would help you to gain more sales.

_____

_____

_____

What content can you provide your customers (on a repeated basis)?

_____

_____

_____

_____

_____

_____

6.   Business Email & Web Strategies, Part II

1.   The Offer

> Best practice companies make their branding
> bold and recognizable.

Best practice companies know that the first hurdle to effective marketing communications is a compelling message in the e-mail subject line. The second hurdle is crafting the offer in a way that the customer:

- Wants to read it
- Immediately grasps two or three key messages that communicate the relevance, legitimacy, timeliness, and value of the offer

To clear these hurdles, best practice companies make their branding bold and recognizable and make sure the offer is:

- Presented near the top of the e-mail message
- Easy and quick to read
- Enticing, with lots of white space and few or no graphical gimmicks that distract the customer from the message
- Linked to more information, enlarged views of graphic images, and offer add-ons for those who want to do more research
- Structured so that the customer can either accept with a click or opt out from the current and future e-mail campaigns

Make sure the recipient's e-mail address is automatically populated on the landing page (more on that topic after we look at suggestions of offers that might work to titillate your audience to interact with you and your website).

There are circumstances in which a gift or being entered into a sweepstakes for a gift is highly effective. These include:

- Marketing to large audience segments where you need to sweep up the maximum response for database development or lead solution activities
- Rewards for attending a seminar or webinar or for stopping at a trade show booth
- Incentives to take a free online demo
- Thank-you gifts for agreeing to speak to or meet with a sales representative
- Free guides, books, white papers, checklists
- Free self-assessments or evaluation tools
- Free planners or calculators

- Free demo disks
- Free audits
- Additional free support or training
- Sweepstakes
- Well-targeted gifts
- "How to" guides (how to evaluate, how to compare)
- Free accessory to a product
- Purchase discounts and rebates
- Free shipping
- Gifts
- Additional products
- Sweepstakes
- Extended warranties

2.   *The Landing Page*

What are you offering your prospects?

When you arrive on a website landing page (a landing page, remember, is simply the specific page that contains relevant information targeted on the sole objective of completing a lead or click-through acquisition or conversion), what's on your mind?

- How much time is this going to take?
- Are they trustworthy?
- Man, that back button is sure looking good right about now.

Expect huge numbers of people to abandon your landing page if you fail to get that eyeball to browse a little longer.

If you can hold a visitor for more than eight seconds, your guest has moved on to the next step: "Should I accept this offer?" This is where your marketing copy and pitch come in. Visitors will scan your intro copy, media content, product information, testimonials, and design value and decide whether or not to convert. If your site is not functional or has usability issues, you can lose conversions. Even not making a "privacy policy" available is risky business, so ensure that it's posted, and that there are no hiccups in form processing.

Here are more simple tips to maximize the success of your next landing page:

- Eliminate unneeded elements. Distractions can kill conversions. This is not your home page. The visitor expects to see something familiar, and since the user has already been screened by your ad, your landing page shouldn't have anything not related to the ad that drew your visitor to it.

- Go one step further. Place the same ad design or image on the landing page. The easiest way to clue visitors that they have arrived at the right place is to use the heading from your ad creative.

- Remove navigation. If you can, remove the navigation bar (unless, of course, it's essential to the conversion process). If a link has nothing to do with your message, toss it!

- Avoid the scroll. Keep your content above the fold. Converting is like herding cats, and scrolling could easily lead your visitor right to the back button and click off. If you have to use a long scroll of text on the page, then remember to place your form or conversion fields at every scroll-and-a-half of screen space

- Use beautiful images. And have a purpose when considering the size of the image and where you place it on the landing page. Big images will demand tons of eye time and if misplaced can ruin the flow of your message. Think of your image as part of a staircase leading up or down to the text and straight to the form field where the user enters an e-mail address and completes the conversion. If the image is of the gift, the offer, the prize, I recommend placing it near your opt-in field. Shopping cart tests have shown consistently 20% higher conversions when a photo of the item is displayed than when it is not. Moreover, tests have proven that placing the image near the register, buy now, or submit button also increases conversions 20% on average.

Here are some simple tips to maximize the success of your opt-in form.

- Walk through this e-mail example trail just as the recipient would: Recipient receives e-mail. Recipient clicks on e-mail. Recipient's e-mail address is visible in a data capture field with a button requesting the recipient click once. Ask yourself, wouldn't you be more likely to click through if your e-mail address was pre-populated (visible without you the user having to enter it again) on that page so all you had to do was click once more to finish your online experience? Virtually anyone you ask will answer yes.

- Fix forms. Meaning, optimize your forms. Make the input cursor hop to the next field after a user finishes the current field. Allow the user to tab around fields. Auto-populate any fields you can.

- Remove all unneeded fields. Don't ask for city/state/province if you ask for a Zip or postal code. Focus on the essentials.

- If you're asking users to register for an e-newsletter, ask for only the e-mail address. You don't need a name now. (I'm not completely against asking for first and last name and e-mail address. Testing these two variations has generated the same amount of leads on my website.)

Here's a good example of applying some of the tactics mentioned above to an e-mail campaign for McAfee, Inc.

McAfee Success Story

Riley Design Associates asked Hart Creative Marketing to collaborate on a complete e-mail marketing campaign for McAfee. The primary campaign goal was to educate McAfee partners about a new Rewards Program in which constituents earned points toward retail merchandise based on the partner's sales volume. However, McAfee also needed to collect information about its partners as a secondary aim. The success of their campaign therefore hinged partially upon the number of constituents that opened their e-mail, clicked through to a landing page and then completed a short series of questions. From the ground up, our e-mail campaign was designed to maximize conversion.

3.   *Measuring Again and Again*

Keep track of everything.

Best practice campaign management, regardless of the channel used to touch the customer (e-mail, direct mail, website, call center), is a closed loop journey: The results of the last campaign are captured, analyzed, and applied to improve return on the next campaign. Such learning requires more than measuring the performance of the campaign, that is, knowing how many customers responded favorably. Part of doing better next time is learning more about the customer. In essence, there are two components to this best practice: (1) enriching individual customer records by (2) conducting post-campaign research.

Best practice companies model the data supporting campaign management by adding new subjects and elements when there is a business need for them. They also tend to acquire or upgrade their data mining and analytic tools to match the knowledge, skills, and abilities of users in marketing as they develop. Here are the types of data and skills that support continuous improvement of campaign management:

Capture and keep detailed information about the customer—what data mavens call granular data. Detailed information can be summarized quickly and flexibly, but summarized data cannot be deconstructed quickly, easily, or cheaply (if at all). Companies that keep detailed integrated customer data derive greater value from it over time because the data can be quickly combined and analyzed to answer new, unanticipated business questions. Summarized data can only answer the business questions that drove the summary report.

Capturing context data is as important as capturing transaction detail. Part of campaign context is data about the offer and the criteria used:

- Modify assumptions
- Analyze results
- Target customers
- Prepare offer
- Plan campaign
- Execute campaign

Generally, consistent customer experience with a company's products and services creates a unique association with the brand, and trust in the brand results when the experience is consistently superior (based on the customer's notion of superiority). Trust in the brand theoretically results in customer loyalty and supports value (as opposed to competitive) pricing. Research indicates that loyal customers will tolerate a 25% price increase for a trusted brand before they consider switching.

Customers who only hear about offers that they perceive to be relevant to their current needs and desires are more likely to consider the company a "trusted advisor" than they would if most offers were irrelevant or mistimed. Demographic information about the individual customer may be very relevant; the less demographic information is tied to the individual, the less value it has for measuring "propensity to buy"—the likelihood a customer will accept the campaign offer.

Summary data (often purchased at a premium from third parties) about age groups, zip codes, and even education levels reinforce stereotypes that may be leaving potential customers out of the segment. At a minimum, marketing cannot refine its ability to target offers unless it can relate demographic detail with purchasing detail about an individual customer.

Poor practice companies tend to build infrastructure and purchase tools that are far beyond the immediate needs and abilities of their end users. As a result, the investment far exceeds business value, and implementation is complex, so business users have to wait for the capabilities and tools they actually need. They tend to treat CRM (customer relationship management), of which campaign management is a component, as a point-in-time project whereas best practice companies treat it as a program that grows and evolves over time.

4.   *Measuring and Predicting*

> Your number one asset is the customer. Know what they like and how they respond.

How well do you know your customers? How often do they buy? What motivates them to make multiple purchases? How can you ensure long-term loyalty? How can you attract and retain new customers?

And, most important, how can you cost effectively align your marketing campaign to ensure that you are sending the most relevant message to each customer segment at the time they are most likely to buy?

The number-one asset of a company is its customers, and a close second is the information about those customers gained through operational customer relationship management (CRM) systems.

Leading marketers have taken advantage of the powerful benefits of sales force automation, call center software, and other CRM systems to identify customer demographics, track purchases, monitor shopping habits, and identify product preferences. As a result, they have been able to maximize the interaction between company and customers, increase sales, and build a loyal customer base.

Managing this wealth of valuable customer information as a strategic asset, however, is what makes the difference between simply tracking customer behavior and capitalizing on that information to understand and optimize the financial value of each customer.

Predicting customer product preferences and purchasing habits, and crafting the most relevant marketing messages around this information, requires a carefully orchestrated mix of intuition and an analytical framework that supports fact-based decision making.

Without an analytical structure in place, even the savviest marketers will have difficulty manually analyzing all of the complex information they may be gathering on customers. And, while still a powerful resource, an operational CRM system alone will struggle to provide the deeper customer understanding required to add value to every interaction with each customer.

Predictive analytics, including data mining, are needed to provide a clear picture of what is going to happen, in order to take the most effective action. The predictive analytic process discovers the meaningful patterns and relationships in data, separating signals from noise, and provides decision-making information about the future.

For example, which customers will be buying what next, or which customers are likely to defect? By supporting CRM with predictive analytics, companies of all sizes can begin to manage customer information as a strategic asset when developing marketing campaigns. Doing so will result in better decisions on what message to send, whom to send it to, and when to send it.

Understand customers

Using typical data-driven segmentation approaches, marketers can easily uncover literally thousands of attributes that define customer behaviors. However, with so much data it becomes too difficult and time consuming to manually process the information for efficient fact-based decision making. Predictive analytics that supports the operational CRM system automatically scans the data and "crunches" it quickly so that marketers can go in to query the results and get specific answers. With the results of the multidimensional customer profiles applied to current marketing campaigns, the interaction with the customer is optimized to be more relevant, more appropriate, and targeted for increased response frequency.

Develop targeted offers
Once marketers gain a deeper understanding of their customers, they can more easily target specific offers to their most profitable customers and promising prospects. Applying predictive analytics to determine customer propensities toward certain product categories enables better decision making in selecting the right products to promote. Moreover, predictive analytics can help marketers to more accurately analyze the results of targeted campaigns, revealing patterns in customer behaviors and preferences that subsequently can be leveraged for unique product offers.

Execute campaigns in real time
With specific messages and marketing channels in place for specific customers, a CRM system enhanced with predictive analytics can achieve real-time customer recommendations. Individual customer predictions, or a model that assigns scores based on customer behaviors, help marketers match the most relevant product offers based not only on the frequency, but also on the complete range of demographic and purchasing behavior data available for each customer. Because the scoring process evaluates past data to forecast the probability of future customer behavior, marketers can tailor their CRM systems to respond with specific offers for specific customers, a strategy proven to increase response rates and optimize the value of each customer.

Match a specific offer to a specific individual
Predictive analytics facilitates propensity modeling, which enables marketers to fine-tune specific messages to specific customers within each marketing channel—e-mail, direct mail, website, call center—and determine what approach elicits the best response. By employing propensity modeling using predictive analytics, marketers can quickly isolate different customer segments and replace a "one-size-fits-all" campaign with an individualized, highly relevant message tailored to the customer's profile that results in a higher response rate.

Monitor campaign results
With predictive analytics in place, the entire CRM process can be monitored to determine whether the current marketing campaign is generating the expected results. Customer metrics can be easily tracked and continually evaluated, providing instant insight into current customer behavior as well as statistically sound calculations to help marketers predict future activity. By keeping a close eye on customer metrics such as sales, retention rate, and churn propensity (the likelihood that current customers may be lost to competitors), marketers can revise marketing campaigns to respond to the customer's actual behavior at any given time and continue to monitor the success or failure of marketing efforts.

Satisfying customers in today's highly competitive global marketplace has never been more challenging. Having a deeper insight into customer expectations and future behaviors is the key to successful marketing campaigns. Predictive analytics enables marketers to understand the key factors that drive customer value and loyalty, and that attract more customers.

5. Enhancing Email Response

You should optimize messaging at each stage of your campaign.

E-mail marketing is a process. It is, among other things, about moving people through a cycle of events. We can look at this cycle from the potential customer's perspective, from three different decision points the customer reaches upon receiving a promotional e-mail message. At our agency we call this cycle, or chain of decision events, "OCC" for Open-Click-Complete. It is a process, so it truly deserves its own acronym.

The objective is to optimize messaging at each stage, or decision point, of this process in order to enhance response, thereby increasing overall campaign results. Accomplishing this requires some creative segmentation capabilities and a little messaging know-how. To illustrate how the process might work, let's look at a simple hypothetical example of a subscription-based company with a house list of nonpaid leads that were garnered by an offer for a free newsletter. The goal is to convert these leads to become subscribers to the company's paid publication.

We develop our first promotion to these folks to get them to pay up. We create a catchy e-mail and landing/transaction page, and even add a worthy premium to the mix. When all is said and done, response rates are so-so, with overall results falling short of our expectations. Rather than sitting on our duffs and trying to analyze the thing to death, we decide to keep chipping away at what we've got in front of us. Using the decision points below as a guide, we realize that we have a ton of information to work with and there still may be life within certain segments of this audience.

Decision 1: To Open or Not to Open
First, let's look at the recipients who never opened the message. This likely represents a huge portion, 50% or more, of the original list. Provided this group is large enough, we pull the nonopeners out and segment them into a few statistically significant cells. We send each cell a new subject line and/or change the sender's, or "from," name or address. What does this do to our open rate?

Chances are good that we'll find some of the changes work better than others, and that some of the nonopeners to the first message have opened up the new message based on a single and possibly simple change. Perhaps this change lies in a new appeal in the subject line, or perhaps it's because the message comes from a living person instead of an impersonal company (or vice versa, depending on how you launched the original message). Record and save those variables and continue to test and fine-tune them with each subsequent campaign.

Decision 2: Shall We Click?

Next we have the segment of the original list that did, in fact, open the message but wasn't interested enough in the offer to click through to the transaction page(s). Again, this could be a sizable group. We realize that some of these folks may not have actually opened the message. Their e-mail program may simply be set to display all incoming messages in preview mode, which will make these recipients report in as "opens." In fact, a good portion of this group may not have had any more interest in the message than the original nonopener group mentioned above. If, indeed, they saw only the previewed message, they may have seen only the top two or three inches of it. Analyze this section of your promotion. Does it say enough to make folks want to read further? If not, reformatting and/or reworking the introductory copy and headline may be all it takes to increase your clicks. If the numbers justify it, test various openings to this group of nonclickers.

Decision 3: Do You Want to Dance?

Next, we have the odd ones, the list members who were interested enough to click through from the e-mail message but decided to jump ship once they hit the offer page. This group obviously won't be as large as the other two groups mentioned above, so testing may not be possible. Take a hard, objective look at that landing page. Something is clearly missing or is not being communicated properly. Does the offer remain clear? Is the form too cumbersome or too long? Can you revise the form, and perhaps also revise some of the required form fields within it, for purposes of having these potential customers complete their first transaction?

Make some assumptions and apply them to your next campaign. It's all about getting potential customers over that hurdle and making that first commitment. Of course, it can get a lot more complex than this. Rather than look at just one campaign, we can create "scores" for each segment, the openers/nonopeners, the clickers/nonclickers, and the converters/nonconverters, and rate them based on how they complete each decision point over a series of campaigns. We can then create customized messages based on the most pertinent previous trends and on how list members interact with each previous message, and can cross-reference those data points with other valuable information we might have within our records, such as RFM (recency, frequency, monetary) data. That's when things start to really get fun. If you're not applying even a bit of creative

segmentation and customized messaging as in the digested
hypothetical example above, think about doing so. Yes, it will take
more time and thought, but the enhanced results you can glean over
a period of time can be well worth it. Bring it on.

6. *The Next Shiny Thing*

Customers are distracted are you the reason?

There's certainly something to be said, generally speaking, for some
shiny things, what we fun-loving, easily distracted humans tend to
go after. In the e-mail realm, they can include promotions that use
animation, voiceovers, video, and Macromedia Flash. Since we're
marketers, we often like to explore so-called sexy tactics like those
that gain our attention. It helps us think of how we can apply them
to grab new eyeballs from our own prospect pools. However, when we
do this, we often lose sight of the fact that we're marketing to people
and not eyeballs. Unique people at that, each with his or her own
internal blueprint that determines all the variables that ultimately
make that person respond. And for many people, both online and
offline, "sexy" just doesn't sell.

I had a conversation recently with a colleague, a bright, ambitious
young woman who was telling me that the only commercial e-mails
that captivate her nowadays are the ones using nifty tricks that take
advantage of the movement and sound this medium offers. She cited
an example: a commercial e-mail with one large and colorful graphic
and headline that, when her mouse scrolled over it, would project an
amusing sound byte intended to sell. Eye-catching and ear-catching?
Yes, but would something like this sell high-ticket investment
newsletters? Would it be helpful in developing a decent number of
good quality business-to-business leads? My colleague suggested
that e-mail marketing agencies like ours might want to create more
promotions of this nature to stay ahead of the game, to remain fresh,
and to ensure that we remain forward thinking. My idea of forward
thinking is keeping an eye on that eight ball. It's not about
constantly coming up with innovative and glamourous ways to reach
our potential customers. It's about maintaining our focus on those
customers, getting inside their heads, and looking in and not out.

In the offline direct marketing world, we see the variances between
the markets, and the "packaging," clearly. After all, on a cost-per-
message basis, direct mail is quite a bit more expensive than e-mail,
so offline marketers have to be darned sure that they are targeting
their prospects properly. For example, you wouldn't see a (smart)
marketer send a three-dimensional-premium-enclosed-lead-
generation package that cost upwards of $30 each to a list of people

126 – Blueprints for Success - eMarketing

that are qualified to receive it just because they're likely to enjoy the premium, would you?

In other words, there's a good chance these folks would open the package to get the gift, but probably wouldn't take the bait on the ultimate objective of the piece, which is to garner new, qualified leads. By the same token, you wouldn't see Nielsen Media's TV ratings service send out mail pieces with silver dollars enclosed ONLY to people who, hey, could use a buck. The marketers at Nielsen need to target people who have televisions at the very least.

On the other side of the coin, the plain-Jane packages from "yesteryear," envelopes with letters enclosed, 28-page booklets on newspaper stock, are still generating millions upon millions of dollars in revenue every year for companies that have historical success using it because these packages are hitting the right markets that respond to these more copy-driven messages, and likely will continue to respond to them as long as there is a desire and a need. Which brings me back to the e-mail space and what we do there.

It's no secret that so many of the markets that we target offline can now be culled online. The so-called high-end target markets from the direct marketing world, the ones that respond to the boring, copy-driven messages mentioned above, are here as well. I'm not saying that if we're working within those markets, we need to send them tomes through e-mail. I am saying, however, that words and the power behind them (embedded, perhaps, in a graphically enhanced HTML promotion) are critical to truly reaching these folks.

When we saturate the e-mail marketplace with "sexy" we dilute its power, and, in my opinion, we hurt our space. While glitz and glamour may have their place, they shouldn't be employed by every marketer. Know your audience and hit their unique hot buttons, which may have nothing to do with anything the least bit shiny.

7. *No Emails? A Letter? Now You're Talking*

How do you communicate with your customers?

Determine the best means to communicate with your audience. That may be e-mail, but it could be regular mail, fax, or other means. Do not simply eliminate other options to save money or time for staff. If you convert to electronic communications, explain the reason(s) for doing so, and transition to e-mail or other formats over time.

Offer alternative means for people to receive information from you. For one organization I chaired, I printed out and mailed every month a paper newsletter to nine members (out of 90) who wanted to receive it by the U.S. mail. They were offered the option of receiving it by regular mail or e-mail, and opted for the former. The remaining members preferred to receive the newsletter by e-mail, and that is what they got.

Provide e-mail recipients an easy way to stop receiving communication from you. That means an unsubscribe line (or simple language letting recipients know they should tell you they do not want the communication) in every e-mail you send to a targeted group, even if the recipient is a client or member who has paid you money to receive your information. Perhaps they consider your communication redundant, the format inappropriate for e-mail, or simply useless, or they simply do not want to hear from you as often as you want to communicate to them.

Adding an unsubscribe message also gives users a way to avoid telling the sender directly that their e-mail is unwanted. I have sensed that some people fear offending list managers when they ask to be removed, in the absence of any language making it easy to cease the communication. An unsubscribe message offers recipients an out and minimizes bruised feelings at both ends of the communication.

Identify the types of information members of key audiences want to receive from you by e-mail. Perhaps it is new product announcements, articles, legislative updates, or meeting notices. On the other hand, perhaps there is content they do not want to receive, like announcements on meetings they would not attend under normal circumstances or multiple reminders to attend these same meetings.

There is blind carbon copy (bcc). By putting a list of recipients in the bcc field within your e-mail software (whether it is Microsoft Outlook, Yahoo, Hotmail, or any others), you hide the individual e-mail addresses from everyone else. So recipients see your message, minus a long string of addresses visible if you simply put everyone in the "to" or cc field. In short, using bcc safeguards the privacy of your correspondents and is a positive step toward keeping your messages short.

8.   *The Touch Point*

What

We all have "skin in the game" of increasing conversions and shortening sales cycles. It directly affects our compensation or bonuses. Organizations spend a lot of time, effort, and money to get prospects to select their product or service. Yet few organizations know the most common sequence of interactions new customers encounter as they move from awareness of a company's offerings through to selection. Understanding these "touch points" that make up your customers' "paths" are critical to increasing conversions and shortening the sales cycle.

So what are these paths? They represent the sequence of touch points that prospects and customers encounter as they travel through their lifecycle stages with your organization.

In our research we have identified four types of paths:

- Initial selection: The sequence of touch points prospects encounter as they proceed from awareness of your offering, to information gathering or knowledge, through to consideration and finally selection.

- Repurchase: The sequence of touch points a repeat customer encounters to repurchase the same product/service.

- Additional purchases: The sequence of touch points a current customer encounters through the process of selecting a different product or service.

- Loyalty/Advocacy: The sequence of touch points a customer encounters that motivates loyalty and/or advocacy.

Your organization probably has thousands of combinations and permutations of touch points customers can encounter along their various paths. Understanding these paths is important because it positions an organization to ease, motivate, and guide travel along these paths, and to even shorten the time it takes to travel the paths. The results? Increased conversion performance over a shorter period of time.

9.   Customer In, Email Out

Set up an automated process to send out email.

E-mail always offers new ways to generate and retain customers. Today, it's a way to help turn website visitors into buyers. This technique works best for a site that sells numerous products, but it can be implemented on sites with any number of items for sale. The assumption is that your e-mail list is permission-based and the addresses were obtained properly under CAN-SPAM guidelines. You have my address on file. I visit your sports memorabilia site, and, because you have my cookie, you can keep track of which pages I visit and which products I've investigated. Site abandonment is extremely high, a big problem for online retailers. Perhaps people abandon your site after browsing because of navigation issues, pricing, product selection, or other factors. In many cases, it has nothing to do with your site. Depending on how well the site is designed, most people leave for other reasons. I might leave your site, but plan to return, for reasons such as:

- I was called into a meeting
- I was interrupted by a phone call
- I had to take the dog out for a walk
- The baby started crying
- I had to take my son to his baseball game
- I lost my internet connection

Visitors leave sites for many reasons beyond your control, but something can be done to get those visitors back. Thanks to the cookie, you know before I left I was looking at a Hank Aaron autographed baseball, a Tom Brady autographed football jersey, and a Hulk Hogan wrestling poster. Most site visitors would be receptive to a follow-up e-mail such as:

Dear (name of website visitor),

Thanks for visiting mysportssite.com yesterday. I noticed you left after spending only a short time on the site. Maybe you were interrupted and couldn't continue browsing.

Let me take this opportunity to give you links to the pages you were looking at, in case you want to come back. They were:

- Hank Aaron autographed baseball:
- http://www.mysportssite.com/products/12903.html
- Tom Brady autographed football jersey:
- www.mysportssite.com/products/13849.html
- Hulk Hogan wrestling poster:
- www.mysportssite.com/products/18594.html

Should you decide to purchase any of these products this week, I'll take an additional 10% off the price. To take advantage, use the following discount code at checkout: 180384. It's effective until Sunday, April 22, at midnight.

Finally, if you'd like to learn more about unadvertised specials and new collectibles, sign up for our newsletter at: www.mysportssite.com/news.html.

Thanks again for visiting. We hope to be of service to you.

Sincerely,

Name
Title
E-mail address

Set up an automated process to send out e-mail a day after someone visits, based on pages viewed. You can customize parts of the e-mail (e.g., slightly different messages for new and repeat visitors) and test various promotions, such as a discount versus free shipping. If 1,000 people browse your site and 980 leave without buying, this is a good way to get them to return.

It's so important to ensure that you receive e-mails from customers after they receive your e-mails, whether from a campaign or simply an auto responder from a touch point on your website. Providing unique inbound e-mail boxes to receive campaign responses can help get customer e-mail regarding the campaign into the right hands faster. However, be prepared for customers who read the campaign, then go to the website to respond and therefore send the campaign-related mail to a different inbound mailbox. Similarly, customers may use the campaign mailbox to submit complaints, suggestions, or questions that have nothing to do with the campaign.

10.   *Managing Inbound Email*

> What are the best practices for handing large amounts of email?

Best practice companies implement procedures, anticipate scaling, and assign responsibility for managing inbound e-mail:

- E-mail handling is centralized for efficiency and effectiveness.

- Business rules differentiate how inbound e-mail is handled, and those business rules are defined and updated by business people, not technical professionals.

- Customers receive an immediate acknowledgment from the company if time is required to answer their questions or resolve the issues raised. Best practice companies develop message templates from which a customer services representative (or a smart agent) selects, perhaps personalizes, and sends to the customer.

- Use filters to organize inbound e-mail, but resist the temptation to rely solely on automation, at least until the marketing department is satisfied that the automated response matches the customer's input every time.

Depending on the company's customer strategy, certain inbound e-mail from customers will always be handled manually, like complaints addressed to the CEO, for example. Filters can be used to redirect such e-mail to an individual or workgroup that will investigate and respond on behalf of the executive. Again, it is imperative that the filter redirect inbound e-mail accurately.

Statistics on inbound e-mail are captured and integrated with other data used to evaluate campaigns and marketing strategy. If your company is concerned with maintaining and enhancing customer relationships, the system will re-sort inbound mail to assure it gets to the person who can act on it. I encountered this problem with a customer who had a third party hosting their e-mail service. Sure enough, when they checked with their provider, they discovered the provider had a policy against bulk e-mail. We were able to deal with the issue before the e-mail contact system went into production.

Checklists

Write a compelling message for one (1) of your products or services. Use the information at the beginning of Chapter 7 to guide you through the process.

_____

_____

_____

_____

_____

_____

What do you want the customer to see when they click to respond to your message (what is on your landing page?)?

_____

_____

_____

Name at least 3 items you could use as a prize for an email campaign.

_____

_____

_____

What customer data do you want to capture for your email campaign?

_____

_____

_____

_____

_____

What facts do you know about your current customers (that has relevant information for creating your email campaign)?

_____

_____

_____

_____

How often do your customers buy from you each year?

_____

_____

Do you have a method for recording and tracking customer purchases?

_____

_____

How do you anticipate tracking your email campaign?

_____

_____

List 5 things you can do to test your email campaign?

_____

_____

_____

_____

_____

What are you doing to back-up your email campaign? (the alternatives)

_____

_____

_____

_____

_____

_____

List all the touch-points you have with your current customers.

_____

_____

_____

_____

_____

_____

NOTES

7. E-Newsletters

1. E-Newsletter Planning

A major part of e-newsletter planning is having a deep working knowledge of your target marketplace before thinking about almost any other strategy element. You have to know whom you want to reach and what their informational needs are and then be prepared to fill those needs.

Getting stringent
Start by identifying the key audience segments of people most likely to buy your products or services. For instance, in the human resources marketplace, segments might be determined by position (corporate human resources, small business management, independent human resources trainer, etc.). Your segments might be further defined by categories, such as customer, prospect, influencer, or channel/reseller.

The next step is to develop audience profile fields for each segment. At the outset, perhaps five to ten specific areas of interests or characteristics that can provide you with insights that will influence strategic marketing decisions down the road. In human resources, these might include concentrations such as leadership development, hiring systems, or workforce retention.

E-newsletters are a lot like dating. If you're really interested in someone, you want to gain that person's attention and trust so that you can continue to engage with each other and you can progress to the next date . . . and beyond.

You can use your e-newsletters to gain the trust of your readers, and then, with this trust, you can get to the next level of engagement and the next until ultimately you lead your qualified readers to a buying decision. Successful e-newsletters, the ones that show you understand your audience, have the recipient's best interest at heart and are capable of delivering solutions for your audience's problems, making people want to do repeat business with you. This type of engagement can be very profitable. In fact, Harvard Business School Publishing states that, with just a 5% increase in customer retention, service industries saw an average of 70% increase in profits. That's one heck of a payback.

Three rules of engagement can lead you to successful reader relationships: target and segment your audience, create a dynamite content strategy, and deploy on the right e-marketing platform.

Know thy audience (segmentation) target market time
Remember, the more targeted your content is, the more you can distinguish customers from prospects, time wasters from interested

parties, and those with the big bucks from those without. I can't stress enough the need to use the data in your database to segment your newsletter. Walk in your readers' shoes and really get a sense for what each segment wants to hear from you. This simple step may take a little extra time, but in the end it will nurture budding relationships and make you smarter and richer.

Remember that as you create an ongoing, engaging relationship with your readers, your newsletter can provide you with a wealth of information. With data from each subscriber encounter, you can, with increasing proficiency, profile audience segments, mine the collected data for valuable marketplace intelligence, follow evolving trends with your readership, and individualize communications and incentives effectively. Here's where to start:

1. **Determine your ideal customer profile.** Develop your target market segments by building a specific audience profile for each. This will help you identify profitable opportunities, areas of growth potential, acceptable risks, and acceptable entry and exit barriers. Target profiles can be built with segmentation variables such as:

   - **Demographics:** age, sex, income, education, race, marital status, household size, geographic location, size of city, job function, intent to purchase, and purchasing authority

   - **Geography:** countries, states, zip codes, telephone numbers, Internet Service Providers, and e-mail services (such as AOL or Yahoo!)

   - **Psychographics:** personality- and emotionally based behavior linked to purchase choices; for example, whether customers are risk-takers or risk-avoiders, impulsive buyers or safe-and-sound purchasers

   - **Lifestyles:** hobbies, recreational pursuits, entertainment, vacations, and other nonworking pursuits

   - **Belief and value systems:** religious, political, nationalism, and cultural beliefs and values

   - **Life stages:** chronological benchmarking of people's lives at different ages (e.g., preteens, teenagers, empty nesters)

   - **Geo-demographics:** people with similar demographics and psychographics living in clusters, or, as the saying goes, "Birds of a feather flock together"

2. **Create a database of your audience segments.** Once you've built your target market profiles, you can start to build a database of e-mail addresses with the data you've collected about each subscriber. You can then segment your readers based on the profile data, crafting your newsletter so it nurtures the individual needs and interests of your readers as well as your existing relationship with them.

3. **Develop audience fields.** Your audience fields can expand over time to provide strategic insights into your readers' purchases and buying influences as your relationship matures. In the technology marketplace, these fields might include existing hardware, software, and networking equipment; plan-to-buy information; or purchase influence or authority.

4. **Complement your existing database.** Based on the target profiles and audience fields you've developed, you can complement your existing database entries with list building and opt-in strategies that include website registration, subscription offers, customer warranty and service cards, and e-mail matching services. Remember that your database is a living, breathing entity—it is constantly evolving and will never be complete.

Beautiful choreography

With this as your starting point, you'll be on your way to choreographing a very successful e-newsletter communication strategy. And, as you'll see in the following pages, you will then be able to create and develop specific content categories and resources that turn your e-newsletter into a custom communication program that helps you keep in touch with your prospects and customers. The more targeted your content, the more you can distinguish customers from prospects, nurture budding relationships, and decide which ones will give you the best return on your investment.

2. Secrets to Writing an Effective E-Newsletter

> Be authentic and be real.

E-newsletters have a bright future. However, it's critically important to be timely and supply specific information in every mailing. We recently studied a successful newsletter from Australia that, every morning, just before the Australian stock market opened, delivered the news of the American stock market. A weather newsletter delivered every morning is another example of the kind of timely and specific information that holds users' attention.

142 – Blueprints for Success - eMarketing

General information such as human interest stories and columns work best in traditional media, but e-mail newsletters must leverage the benefits of new media, instant transmission, and narrowcasting. You can have a market that's a tiny segment and be high value for that. If newsletters don't give timely and useful information, the consequences could be deadly.

Survey results suggest that users have a zero-tolerance attitude for anything that wastes their time. And they often hit the spam button to delete newsletters instead of unsubscribing. This is bad for e-mail publishers because if too many people say you are sending spam, services like Yahoo! and MSN's Hotmail are not going to deliver your newsletters to anyone. This also increases the importance of making it easy to unsubscribe to newsletters.

According to a recent survey, subscribers' top four peeves were too-frequent mailings, irrelevant content, newsletters for which they had not signed up, and finally, ads that led to sites with pop-ups. If you are going to link your newsletter, make the landing page someplace of interest and don't use pop-ups. Make a simple, clean landing page that follows up on your ad.

The big challenge in distributing an e-mail newsletter is generating content that will motivate prospects to open, read, and respond to your newsletter. Writing the articles is a funny topic to me, as many editors of an e-newsletter usually wait until the last minute to start development when there is a much better way. Every day, you probably run into all kinds of valuable content that can be saved in a folder and retrieved when you're ready to build your e-newsletter. The following are examples of useful content:

- How to solve common problems that your prospects might face
- How your prospects can take advantage of recent technological developments
- Industry news and trends
- Case studies of how others have improved their operations

The information in the newsletter should come from the experts in your company such as executives, engineers, scientists, sales representatives, customer support representatives, and so on. Your customers will love to get comfortable with your mailings, accepting and probably enjoying relevant and timely information that they come to expect on a regular basis.

The problem with someone internal doing the writing is that these people are typically very busy. Furthermore, because they aren't experienced writers, they usually take a huge amount of time to produce a product that, despite their best efforts, doesn't do a very good job of communicating.

What I suggest initially when launching an e-newsletter is finding an experienced writer who can extract your experts' knowledge in a short interview and then generate professional-quality copy at an economical cost. Most people never take this route and the results can be devastating. You've heard that statement, "It's all about presentation." Presentation is the use and placement of words that speak to your recipient. Those words will generate a positive feeling of "I love it," or the content may not be as relevant and your reader will "shove it," which pretty much means delete. That's a high price to pay if you lack the writing skills to captivate your audience. This is not an area where you want to exercise your ego or arrogance.

Make it interesting
I don't know who started the rumor that significant and profitable businesses must also be serious and boring, but it seems to have caught on nonetheless. That's good news for you and me because with all the dry e-newsletters out there trying to sound like the front page of the Wall Street Journal, we can make our newsletters shine with little effort.

Personal anecdotes, conversational language, and the occasional joke here and there will keep your readers involved long enough for them to hear the "real" information you're trying to give them. This formula can also be found in common use on your favorite radio or television show. Take a moment and notice when you're enjoying the show. That's usually when the content is interesting. Take that seriously. Your e-newsletters are no different. Your recipients probably won't read it just because it's interesting, but they certainly won't read it if it's not.

Make it simple
An effective newsletter isn't a doctoral thesis; it's not even a case study. It's what I like to call "a kiss." It's one insight or tip or concept that your readers can take in, understand, and hopefully remember long enough to put into practice. If you give too much information (even if it's good) too often, the reader is likely to gather a collection of your newsletters until deleting them all at once in a frenzy thinking, "I'll never get around to reading these old ones anyway." Give your readers something small enough to understand and remember.

Make it authentic
Done right, your e-newsletter is the voice of your company. It reflects your spirit, unique personality, and culture, whatever that happens to be. I've worked with enough companies to know that each of them, even the ones in seemingly perfect, hard to differentiate industries, have a spirit that can be translated to a message that can be delivered in an e-newsletter.

3.   *Make your E-Newsletter Sell*

Highlight your customers and see what happens.

How do you truly know that your e-newsletter is the most effective and relevant source for delivering value to your list of recipients? Well, it really depends on your goal. If you're writing your e-newsletter as a communications and update tool, you'll measure your success by the kind of feedback you get. Messages from your readers like "I enjoyed your article. Where can I find more on that subject?" will be enough to make your day. Knowing your e-mail was deleted after all the work you put forth to stay in touch would not make your day. The point here is that in the age of epidemic ADD, your shot at holding one's interest is in the shortest of supplies. Is your content timely, tight, bright, and titillating? Even literate people skim and don't read properly because they are so busy.

If the goal of your e-newsletter is to sell your product or service, then you're looking for a different reaction to your content: a purchase, immediately or in the not-too-distant future. Once you get in the habit of providing valuable information that fits your company's business, you'll find it easy to unobtrusively slip in a sales message that will be likely to catch your prospects in a very receptive frame of mind.

Newsletters that simply provide a recap of the latest products and news from the company that sent them will be read only by the most loyal of customers. To reach out and influence potential buyers, you need to provide objective information that can help your prospects do a better job.

Three major components are woven into the success of an e-newsletter: Content, Community, and Commerce. Remember them? At the height of the dot com boom, the three C's were the value proposition of every internet business plan for a sticky website or portal. When those three C's are integrated into your e-newsletter, you'll begin to see your content take shape into something easy to understand and enjoy for both you and the reader of your e-newsletter.

Digestible content
First, the content of your e-newsletter should be useful and relevant to your audience. One of the reasons a reader will abandon your e-newsletter is irrelevance. The price to pay is high for not deeply understanding what's of interest to your customers and prospects. It should be presented in digestible bites, in which the readers are offered a link at the end of your article that directs them to a page where they can complete the reading of that respective content or article.

Think of your e-newsletter as a billboard with cars passing it on the information superhighway. You only have them for a brief moment and can only hope they remember you and maybe even call you or, better yet, come into your office or store.

Your e-newsletter is no different. You flash an e-newsletter billboard by e-mail and you hope your content is relevant enough to engage your recipient to click through and come to your store, meaning the most desired destination, your website. The e-newsletter is the conduit, the bridge for your readers to enter your website with purpose.

Look at one of our most traditional forms of media, the newspaper. The front page is a good example of knowing the customers deeply. If they say too much on the front page, the risk of losing a reader is much higher, ultimately leaving advertisers who have paid for their ads beyond the front page at a greater risk of readers not seeing their ad.

Translation? Those ads in the newspaper following the front page are your website. This is your critical opportunity to have e-newsletter recipients click to finish, viewing an article on your website where you can up-sell them, cross sell, and learn more about their needs.

Creating a feel-good community
The word community is often thrown around like a rubber thong in a discount bin.

Not good, considering community is what drives the spirit of a company. When you can create a culture, a buzz, and an energy of family inside your e-newsletter, you'll unleash one of the single most powerful forces on the internet, community. We do call the net the world wide web, a community of people who can instantly communicate with one another anywhere in the world and do so affordably. That may be too lofty, yet that is the core of the internet's purpose—to bring together the world under one roof, so that we may learn from one another and better understand all of our differences and discover new opportunities.

That buzz of community amongst the recipients of your e-newsletter is a "feeling." They should feel that they've made a wise choice by opening your latest e-mail; that five minutes of reading time yielded an insight or best practice tip to use that day or tuck away for the next project.

A great way to build community is to highlight customers who had a problem, found you, and can proudly say you have the solution. Not just a testimonial, but also a down home story, quite possibly with audio as well, of how you stepped up and filled a need for one of your customers. This creates a sense of community, along with a distinctive, one-to-one voice. In fact, your most loyal readers may be contributing to your community by sending regular feedback or writing a guest article.

Create a chat room or a community where readers can add comments, suggestions, and opinions too, and be amazed at what kind of community you can create amongst your readers. No one likes to feel left out. Much like any group of people crowded in one place, everyone else wants to know, "What's going on over there?" When you see your readers wanting to be a part of your active extended family, you'll become aware of how important "community" can be to building a list of fans that you can e-mail regularly.

Commerce: propelling your reader to become a customer

Finally, you must clearly present your subscribers with buying opportunities. If they know and trust you and your organization, they'll purchase from you, right?

Unfortunately, it doesn't always work that way. Good feelings are not enough to prompt a purchase through an e-mail. You have to create a sense of urgency, a gotta-have-it-right-this-minute proposition.

This is where it takes some experimenting. Maybe you need to offer your newsletter readers a low-priced loss leader. Get them to cross the threshold from reader to customer just once, and you can up-sell them later.

To sell product or services from your e-newsletter, bottom line, you need a formula to add up the three C's properly.

Fanatical consistency

Be "absolutely fanatical" about publishing every week, including Christmas and New Year's. Thus, both the schedule and content of your e-newsletter are predictable. Readers know what to expect and when to expect it.

When I was on the radio, listeners came to expect many tidbits of content at the same time, every day. When I changed, they would become upset and ask me, "Please don't change the time you broadcast the news." Why? Because that was their clock, not the numbers on the real clock—my benchmarked newscast was a way for my listeners to figure out if they were on schedule or had a few more minutes to spare before having to get out of bed and start their day. Your e-newsletter is no different. Take your consistency very seriously. If you're late or miss a month of sending content, you're more likely to damage your credibility, your brand, and worst of all, potential sales.

Problem equals product

By listening carefully to feedback and questions from your subscribers, you'll know what problems they are facing. Readers get bored if you promote the same product week after week. They have different problems they want to solve so you have to have different products that offer a variety of solutions. Look at it simply as stating problems people deal with in their lives and attaching those problems to a product you'd like to sell. If you have 100 products in your online store or on your website, you have 100 problems you can offer free advice to and up-sell your reader from there. One of my clients offers CD's (derived from her teleseminars). That's over 100 problems she can offer free advice to in her e-newsletter.

This may help you further: extract three to five content tips from a product. When planning an issue of your e-newsletter, select a product you want to promote. Extract from it three to five content-rich tips that people can use and benefit from even if they never want to spend a penny with you. Then, write a mini article (200–300 words) incorporating those tips.

Pair content with promotion

You can pitch the product in a short paragraph of 100 words or less. Use a lead-in such as "Need more help solving this problem? Need more ideas? Check out [product title]." Then link to that specific product page on your site. When the reader arrives on that web page, surround the product with testimonials of people who have fallen in love with the product or service that you're offering.

You may also bundle several products together or offer a special 20 to 30% off promotion. Make sure your writing is clear and succinct. When you make the "ask," it must come across as a natural progression of the content preceding it. There's no hard sell. Your e-newsletter may be similar to the "billboard," the tool that bridges your customer or prospect to your website; however, educate and share knowledge first in your e-newsletter and watch your sales grow!

In a nutshell, the secret formula: free advice paired with a product equals revenue, a more attached prospect, or a customer who is deeply connected to your brand, your offers, and your community.

4.   Move Them Through the Sales Cycle

Drive your readers offline.

Not only can you identify your readers by their specific e-mail addresses, but you can also learn how they interact with your newsletter. Your sales reps will go wild when they get this information. You can become a hero by delivering a new prospect right to the sales rep's office door. Here's your opportunity to deliver, big time.

Learn who your sales prospects are

If your newsletter has a good reporting system, you can learn who's reading what and how much time they spend with your newsletters. Readers may be prospects who are already in a sales cycle with one of your reps.

Picture telling a representative, "Joe, you know that big prospect you're trying to get? Well, he read this article on product X and kept coming back to it. Have you talked to him about this yet? Maybe you want to send him that new data sheet." Imagine the possibilities.

Cross-sell to current customers

Perhaps you have a customer who owns product Y. You find out, through his readership patterns, he's frequently expressed an interest in product Q. That little tidbit could be highly beneficial to the sales reps on this account. The customer is telling you, through his interactivity with the newsletter, he has an interest in this product. This is something sales representatives can capitalize on.

Move prospects through a sales cycle

Once you find interested prospects, demonstrated either by readership patterns or through data from your sales teams, you can create a special newsletter intended to move the prospect into the sales cycle. Focus on customer stories highlighting successful product use, or segment prospects by industry and show how your product can make their lives easier, in respect to their own industry.

Generate quarter-end/year-end revenue

A newsletter is a great way to generate revenue from low-hanging fruit. If people were considering buying your product but wanted additional incentive, a newsletter can deliver that message quickly and efficiently. Send a special promotional newsletter with a "buy now and save money" message. You'll drive in some revenue that might otherwise have been delayed until the next quarter.

Send personal messages from your sales reps

Nurture customers and prospects along by personalizing your regular newsletter. Segment your list by sales reps, and send newsletters out with the rep's name in the sender line. You can even include a message from that rep, along with the rep's photo. Customers and prospects will think they're getting a very directed, personal message, and a new communications avenue will open up for your reps. Make sure your reps know you're doing this and that they are on the distribution list.

Send personal messages according to job function

In the midst of a sales cycle, each job function looks for different proof points. A CFO may want to see a return on investment (ROI) justification. A CIO may want to understand how seamlessly your product integrates with her existing systems. Create segmented and highly targeted messages like these by versioning your newsletters.

Offer more information through webinars, white papers, case studies, and the like.

Measure reader interaction over time
With certain tracking tools, you can follow a customer's or prospect's interaction with your newsletter issue by issue. You can tell if certain readers are interacting more or less often over time, providing yet another measure of their viability as prospects. This is an additional way to see how interested they are in your company and products.

Drive your readers offline
You're probably scratching your head over this one, but let's be realistic. We're talking about moving a customer or prospect from the point of identifying a need to where the cash register rings. It's often a long journey that most likely won't be accomplished with use of newsletters alone.

Newsletters, however, do drive clicks. If you can get readers to e-mail a sales rep or get them to a webinar or event (e.g., a trade show) that will further educate them, you've accomplished your goal. They're moving along the chain.

5.   *Learn From the Metrics*

> Always give the prospect a reason to click.

A click-through is only the first response step in permission-based e-mail. Next steps involve getting the recipient to take action toward your ultimate goal, building a relationship and positioning yourself as a partner who can fill their needs. Sometimes this takes one step, sometimes many. It's measuring all these steps that helps you understand your readers' behavior. Ultimately, this will reveal how successful your campaign is. Luckily, there are lots of ways to collect this information.

Direct mail on steroids
eMarketing is center stage on marketing agendas. Electricity surrounding eMarketing is well deserved, especially in a world where return on investment (ROI) must be justified for a program to survive. Think about it: eMarketing is direct mail on steroids. You can drill down right to the value proposition and understand who's buying it, who's not, and why. With this information, you can serve up strong, dynamic programs that build loyal, long-lasting relationships (with great ROI, I might add). If you don't take the time to dig deeply, to learn what your readers' interests and motivations are, you'll end up not only wasting a lot of money but also sending meaningless content. Guess what: that's S-P-A-M!

Behavioral metrics rule

There's a whole lot of data-gathering power in eMarketing, especially with e-newsletters. The result is a new calibration of behavioral metrics that help define, identify, and extract information on how your business can compete better in today's dog-eat-dog business environment.

The right reporting, analysis, and data-mining skills enable you to measure things unimaginable just a few years ago. Here are a few forward-thinking metrics you can consider:

- **Who reads your newsletter? Who doesn't?** This metric helps determine initial usage benchmarks. Ultimately, it reveals who are your best prospects and customers.

- **What does each subscriber read? In what order?** These stats provide insight on what marketing initiatives attract the most engaged, and possibly the most profitable customers. You'll get a hierarchy of readers' interests and begin to understand what drives their reading and purchase behaviors.

- **How long are your readers' sessions?** Reader intensity translates into how interested and brand loyal your readers are. Shorter sessions could mean an unengaged subscriber. This should be a red flag that you may be one step away from being perceived as spam.

- **What do they bookmark?** If readers return numerous times to the same article or page, it's likely they bookmarked it. Note what is of enough value to make them want to come back repeatedly.

- **What's the pass-along/refer-a-friend trend?** Another indication of high personal interest, referring friends or passing an article along, may help you develop a new channel you hadn't thought about earlier. Find out what they pass along and to what type of people. Tap into the viral nature of your communications.

- **What was your reader's click stream?** Did readers open the newsletter, read one article, and then come back later to read the remaining content? Or did they read the promotions first? Did they take an action, like registering for a seminar or buying? By understanding readers' behavior as they engage with your newsletter, you can take your relationship with them to a whole new level.

Complete the circle of engagement
You can weave what you learn from the above metrics into your evolving, living database to build a more effective communication strategy and interactive brand connection. Sharpening your profiling will give you better, more granular segmentation that becomes the cornerstone of strong, personal, one-to-one brand connections. You should continue to mine data to find new insights into evolving trends and reader interests. Use this to align content with readers' preferences and needs. Create stories and articles that are meaningful to subscribers and publish content in a hierarchy built on individual reader history.

Remember, even the most powerful capabilities and technologies are only as good as you make them. Plan carefully, analyze strategically, and when you publish the next edition do it all over again.

Is there an average click-through rate? Question: Is there an average click-through rate or range to judge whether response was poor, average, or good? My good friend and colleague, VP of Marketing for E-maillabs, has nicely defined the averages in this highly questionable area of click-through rates.

Answer. The click-through rate (CTR) is important because without it, you don't get conversions. However, there's no single benchmark click-through rate, because CTRs depend on many factors: whether you send to a business or consumer audience, the kind of mailing you send, how relevant it is to your audience, how often you send, your opt-in process, your use of personalization and segmentation and dozens of other factors. And most significantly, how many links you have in your e-mail and, if you are providing content such as articles, whether you include the entire article within the body of the e-mail or you have a teaser or snippet that requires subscribers to click through to a Web site to read.

Beyond that, many companies calculate and report CTRs differently—using total rather than unique clicks. Many subscribers will click on multiple links, which means that CTRs based on "total" clicks are typically about two times higher than those based on "unique" clicks.

That being said, below are some ranges for average CTRs for permission-based house lists. CTRs that we cite are based on unique clicks (only one click per person is counted) and are calculated as unique clicks/e-mails delivered:

- B2B newsletters typically range from 5 to 15%. If yours are consistently below that level, then among other things, you are probably providing content of little value to your subscribers. Or you may have most of the content within your e-mail, not giving subscribers a reason or means to click through to your site.

- B2C promotional e-mails often range from about 2 to 12%. E-mails with less than a 2% CTR may be a result of overmailing and questionable opt-in processes.

- Highly segmented and personalized lists (B2B and B2C) are often in the 10 to 20% CTR range. Also, e-mail messages with very strong content but sent to unsegmented lists, like many news or trend-type newsletters, are often in the 10 to 15% range.

- Trigger or behavior-based e-mails (e-mails that are sent to a recipient based on some behavior they showed, such as clicking on a product link, visiting a specific Web page, etc.) are often in the 15 to 50% range.

If your e-mails are typically showing under, say, 2 to 3% CTRs, the causes likely include:

- Poor permission or opt-in processes. This includes pre-checked boxes, not making it clear what type of e-mail they will be receiving, automatically adding someone to receive your e-mail when they've actually signed up for something else such as a whitepaper, etc.

- Poorly written subject lines that do not direct and motivate recipients to take an action.

- Poor delivery rates. If a lot of your e-mails are getting blocked or filtered and you don't know it, your CTR will obviously be affected.

- Poor open rates. If few people open your e-mail, fewer recipients have a chance to click.

- Poor design and layout. If they can't easily find where to click through or aren't motivated to by your layout—you've got trouble in River City.

- Lack of links. Quite simply, the more links the better. Make it so that readers are continuously stumbling over text and graphic links like they do signage in a retail store.

No reason to click. If your newsletter has a single or multiple articles in their entirety, then don't expect them to click. You haven't given them any reason. If you are sending a promotional e-mail and you don't include a deadline for the offer, or convey a discount, special offer, limited supply, etc., few people are probably going to take action

6.   *Think Deadline, Think Fun*

> The discipline involved in the success of a newsletter program is one to be noted.

What a surprise when my deadline for launching my upcoming e-newsletter is tomorrow and I have nothing ready to go. What does that say to your audience, your fans, your potential customers, and those passive members of your database that come to expect your e-newsletter on the same day at the same time each month? When you miss your delivery date because you weren't ready, that usually means you lost the discipline. My goal is to help you minimize the threat of the word "discipline." When I repeat that word back to myself, I hear expectation, guilt, and pressure, all the wonderful feelings that will often leave you fatigued and with little creativity to construct your e-newsletter in less than a day's time.

First, we want to limit the frequency with which you face this cumbersome task of completing an e-newsletter on the fly. Why? The best e-newsletters are given fair time to find, integrate, and tweak the content before departure to your database of impressionable people. Do not underestimate how quickly your quality will diminish when you fail to plan. (Of course, you'd never plan to fail, would you?)

The discipline involved in the success of a newsletter program is one to be noted. Not only self-discipline, but also a kind of military precision you, the publisher, must inflict on others.

Here are some insights on how to make discipline work for you:

- **Strategy development**. Be strict with yourself on this one. Consider developing a strong strategy as a gift to yourself, an opportunity to build a strong infrastructure that will last. This involves meeting initially with anyone who cares what your newsletter looks and reads like. What does the CEO want to achieve with the newsletter? How does sales use it as a tool? How do the product marketing and development teams envision using the newsletter? Create a list of common objectives that fulfill overall company goals. Use this as your monthly checklist to make sure your newsletter hasn't wandered off course.

- **Sections**. Your life will be much easier if you create a standard list of sections, or buckets, you use every month. How does this involve discipline? Along the way, you'll get lots of great new ideas for the newsletter. Your first instinct will be to jump on them. Instead, file them away for two or three months. Discipline yourself to keep on track. You spent a lot of time developing strategy, and you didn't go down the path you're on lightly. Stick with it for a while.

- **Editorial calendar**. Don't wait until the last minute to decide what's going into the next couple of issues. Sit down right after you determine the sections and develop as comprehensive an annual calendar as possible. Things will change (that's a promise), but the more you map out the newsletter for yourself and those working with you, the less dictatorial you'll need to be.

- **Deadlines**. Everyone has way too much work and very little time to complete the work they're responsible for. Since you've become a strict disciplinarian, establish clear, hard, and fast deadlines for what's needed. Communicate these to all involved and build in reminders. You can include a grace period for emergencies, but if people use the back-up date too frequently, you have a problem. If management bought into the importance of this project, you may need to be the bad guy and request assistance getting things in on time.

- **Team selection**. Choose your team wisely. If you work with someone who's a great contributor but unreliable with deadlines, you have a couple of options. Give such persons their own, much earlier deadline. Talk with them frankly and ask them to tell you whether they're too overcommitted to participate. If they claim they aren't, yet continue to miss deadlines, even after a prod from you, you'll have to politely, but firmly, let them go.

- **Reporting and analysis.** I'm sure when every issue goes out the door, you'll heave a great sigh of relief, then groan as soon as you realize you must start on the next issue tomorrow. Don't forget the key interim step: Learn from what you publish. Build sufficient time into your plan to figure out what works and what doesn't. Ideally, you can develop a template for summarizing what happens with each issue. Quickly plug in new statistics and see what trends will either help sales now or give strategic direction over time.

Flexibility. Discipline may sound like a rigid word, but even the strictest disciplinarians permit flexibility. Step back every so often and look at what's working and what isn't. Recognize what needs to be fixed or when an absolutely brilliant suggestion walks through the door, if it's worth incorporating today—even if it throws your schedule amuck.

7.   *The Art of Discipline*

Set yourself apart and don't look like everyone else.

The role that discipline plays in the success of an e-newsletter program is more about self-discipline, requiring almost a military-like version of yourself and the guidelines you must inflict on others. Here are some insights on how to make discipline work for you:

- **Be accurate.** Whatever claims you make, benefits you offer, or statistics you quote, make sure they are true and not inflated. Nothing is worse than starting off a relationship with exaggerated or even false information.

- **Be brief.** Your job with e-mail is to capture interest, then provide more information if it's wanted. You need to identify the most important benefit to the recipient and sum it up in a short paragraph. Think of it as the 30-second "elevator pitch" in e-mail form.

- **Be clear.** Most business people are turned off by e-mail messages with bad grammar, misspellings, and/or unintelligible content. If you personally struggle with writing, hiring a professional writer to prepare your messages is a worthwhile investment.

- **Be genuine.** Forget the hype that works with consumers. Your business relationship is built on trust. Make sure everything you say conveys you as a genuine, upstanding, honest person running a reputable business.

- **Speak their language.** Whatever you're going to say, write it in words that they are comfortable with and that they understand. Don't write down to them or above their comprehension level. People tend to understand and react better to words they use in everyday conversations.

- **Put yourself in their shoes.** Try to picture the daily routine of the people you're contacting and reflect that in your writing: "I know you're busy, so I'll get right to the point."

- **Watch out for a "knowledge gap."** Don't assume recipients have the same knowledge about your product or service as you do. After you've captured their interest and have reached the "additional information" stage, try offering a step-by-step walkthrough of whatever you're marketing to help them understand what you're trying to say.

- **Write business e-mails as letters, not as ads.** In the B2B world, a forthright communication in letter format is much more effective than an e-mail that looks and smells like an ad.

- **Take your time:** Let your e-mail message sit for a day or two after you complete it. Show it to colleagues and other business people, and get their opinions. In almost every case, the passage of time and other people's input will help you improve your messaging and writing.

- **Remember your e-mail is likely to be passed around.** Because it's so easy for e-mail to be forwarded, assume your message will be sent to others if the initial recipient has any interest. You may want to include links to information that is relevant to others, including technical details, operations info, and financial data.

- **Mimic your verbal presentation.** Although a lot of what you say in person may not be necessary or appropriate for an initial e-mail, you should still consider how you verbally present your product or service, whether by phone or in person. Think about what points you stress (those could be underlined or bolded in your e-mail) and the words you use (stick with verbal explanations that people understand).

- **Check your signature block.** Make sure it's complete: your full name, title, company, address, phones, pager, fax, e-mail address, and website address. Give the recipient a choice of how to contact you for more information.

- **Carefully choose when you actually send the e-mail.** Most business people spend Monday mornings catching up on the e-mail, postal mail, and phone calls that have piled up since the previous Friday. You don't want your e-mail mixed in with dozens or even hundreds of communications that are being reviewed by recipients.

- **Prepare your subject line carefully.** After the sender address, the subject line is the first thing e-mail recipients will look at. It's akin to what you might say on the phone in the first five to ten seconds. The subject line should directly relate to the primary benefit your product or service offers.

- **Use graphics wisely.** Business people are interested in benefits, details, other customers, and so forth. Unless graphics enhance your message in a meaningful way, don't use them.

- **Make sure links within your e-mail display and work properly.** When you list "for more information" links, make sure they are clickable so the recipient does not have to cut and paste. Also make sure they go to the exact page you want and that the page is up to date and provides the information you want them to have. Sending people to the homepage and leaving it up to them to figure out where to go is a potential lost sale.

- **Be wary about sending attachments.** Most of the time, you don't know what software the recipient has or what filter settings are enabled. Sending PDFs, Word documents, or Excel spreadsheets may not be a good idea, since you don't know if the recipient can read, or even receive, what you send. A better idea is to send links to web pages where the information contained in the attachments is displayed.

- **Test.** Just as you do with any consumer e-mail campaign, test subject lines and message copy. Testing is no less critical with B2B e-mails.

- **Be complete.** Most e-mail recipients will form some sort of preliminary conclusion about your product or service before they respond to your e-mail. They'll determine for themselves whether your e-mail helps meet their needs. That's why providing details and complete information is important in order to give recipients the details they need to make the decision to call you or act on your offer.

Don't look like everyone else. Spend some time reviewing other e-newsletters and see what others are doing. Get on the e-mail lists of your competitors so you can see how they communicate. Analyze them all and find ways to differentiate yourself from the pack.

8. *Grow Your Email List*

> Make growing your e-mail list a part of your routine.

Your e-mail list is one of your most valuable assets. Unless you've got a major brand and a big budget to spend on this initiative, the first thing you must have is *patience*. In e-newsletter publishing, patience is a virtue few of us nurture, and a good, quality subscriber list doesn't happen overnight. You can build a list quickly, but not a quality one.

A very important clarification that may come as a shock: You don't want, or need, to add everyone and his brother to your list. In this case, bigger is not better. In fact, you want to weed out individuals who don't meet your own defined, stringent criteria for receiving your newsletter.

By collecting e-mail addresses and permission on your homepage, and everywhere else, you can take advantage of every opportunity to solidify your existing customer relationships and turn one-time visitors and prospects into your best customers.

Here are some tips to help you accelerate your list building efforts:

Use a signup box
One easy way to collect e-mail addresses and permission is via a signup box on your website. Place your signup box in a visible place on your homepage, and other appropriate pages, where visitors might choose to opt-in. Make sure it's easy for site visitors to find and sign up to join your e-mail list. Notice I said, "easy to sign up."

Don't just do what I suggested, but go one step further. What that means specifically is always giving back to your customers before you expect them to give. Give them an offer with some urgency behind it and a call to action. For example, why not offer a visitor to your website a whitepaper, a free consultation, or a short clip of audio from a recent speaking engagement or seminar. People love when you extend the olive branch. In return, you'll usually see much higher click-through and e-mail submission rates. Always, remember WIIFM. What's in it for me, the customer? Think, why would I just assume that anyone stepping into my website would give me his or her personal mailing address, or e-mail, simply because I placed an empty box that read "join my list"? Well, that's a good start, but a lousy finish.

It's a free offer, urgency, call to action and then BOOM! You can sit back and watch your click-through rates soar.

Start a guest book
In the flesh-and-blood physical world, if you already have a guest book, make sure it includes room for an e-mail address! Place your guest book prominently in your office or store and remind employees to ask customers if they would like to receive your newsletter, special promotions, or notification of private sales and events.

Sloppy writing can increase the number of e-mails that never reach their destination. Why? Your customer or prospect who was in your brick and mortar store provided inaccurate information on the guest list. Some companies, especially retailers who see loads of traffic walking up to point of sale, have installed a computer with keyboard so customers minimize mistakes when entering their e-mail address on the computer.

When using paper, your ratio of customers who provide inaccurate e-mail addresses is about 1 in 10. That may be intentional too. Some may feel obligated to provide their contact data, and then as they are doing so, decide to give you a bad address to avoid any future e-mail transmissions from you. Not bad, but still annoying.

Add a "join our mailing list" link

Place a "join our mailing list" link in the signature of every e-mail you send to clients, business associates, friends and family. The link should go to your home page or the most appropriate page of your site where your signup tag is prominently displayed.

Forward e-mail to a friend

When you send a campaign, you can include a "join our mailing list" link in all forwarded e-mails. This means that when your e-mail gets passed along to others, they can join your list on the spot. However, add a welcome gift as part of the offer for any new member of your list. Offer money off your first service or purchase when this new e-newsletter referral wants to start doing business with you.

More tips to grow your list:

- Set up strategic alliances with complementary companies to cross-promote each other's mailing lists.

- Get current subscribers to refer friends or colleagues. Ask them to forward your newsletter to colleagues with similar interests.

- Create co-registration using a co-registration network or similar complementary publication.

- Create a pop-up window with a subscription box. Pop-ups (and pop-unders) do work and will get more people to subscribe. Employ these carefully so you don't annoy site visitors. Boxes should be intelligent enough to pop up once per user, not every time a user visits the site.

- Optimize your newsletters and its key topics with search engines and crawlers so people conducting searches on topics related to your products or services will find your newsletter.

Make growing your e-mail list a part of your routine. Train sales, customer service representatives, and other employees to collect e-mail addresses and permission at every point of contact:

- On customer service, sales, and support calls.

- On coupons, invoices, statements, brochures, customer surveys, and feedback forms.

- In conjunction with other marketing efforts like radio, print, direct mail, or television advertising.

- At tradeshows or events.

You won't believe how quickly your e-mail list can grow.

9. *What's In It For Them (Wiifm)*

> Subscribers are seriously selfish.

Add a "join our mailing list" link—add it to a home page or an e-newsletter

I've suggested you place a "join our mailing list" link on your website and a link in the signature of every e-mail you send to clients, business associates, friends, and family. The link should go to your home page or the most appropriate page of your website. Now the real strategy begins, in which you stop expecting your web visitor to sign up for your e-newsletter, because you were kind enough to offer a field to type in an e-mail address on your site. Do you know if this visitor has seen your e-newsletter? Statistics show that when visitors to a website or e-newsletter (possibly forwarded from someone on your list) have an opportunity to sign up for an e-newsletter or join a list, they are 50% more likely to follow through and provide an e-mail address if an offer prefaces your request for that oh so valuable information, their e-mail address and hopefully even more.

The landing page for e-newsletter signups

A landing page is a secondary page that users click to once they visit your homepage. For example, I'm not on a particular company's e-newsletter list, but I've been sent an e-newsletter by a friend of mine and I'm interested in what I've received, so now I'd like to see the website to learn more about the company behind the e-newsletter. When I arrive, my eyes are drawn to a box that says "join our list." Why should I? Just because I happened to find some value in your e-newsletter isn't enough of a reason. Where is the offer? If you have one, your ratio of conversion of visitors to qualified prospects will double instantly. This special technique is often overlooked and it's one of the strongest and most persuasive ways to build your list and limit the chance of losing a visitor to your website, never to return again. The offer must have a value, and that is in the eyes of the receiver. Too often, I see what you think is of value and I can bet your community of e-mail recipients think "Thanks, but no thanks."

Develop an e-book (or series of e-books) that provides comprehensive and useful information to people who would be interested in your product or service. Feature this document on the home page of your website and in your other promotional material. When visitors click on the link for the e-book, direct them to a landing page that asks them to register for your e-newsletter.

If possible, offer either an inexpensive incentive or a chance at a drawing for a larger prize as an incentive to register. Even better, use this special opportunity to ask for more than just an e-mail address—offer interactive surveys on relevant topics or quick polls on how readers are using your products.

I'm very proud of what we've done at hartcreativemarketing.com, understanding you must give to get. Give value in exchange for anyone allowing us to stay in contact, send permission-based, exciting e-mail messages and hopefully continue to send to an opt-in recipient for years to come.

What constitutes a valuable offer
Offers that stimulate, titillate, and are user friendly in their accessibility are the real winners. This analogy may be silly, but it's effective: I never buy Cracker Jacks for the toy. Same deal on the homepage of your website. If I'm buying into trusting you with my name on your list, then offer me a "feel good," "taste good," "instant gratifier" that's easy to access on your site. A promotion, incentivized discounts, an educational morsel of content, even as much as $100 off a first purchase. Just like those Cracker Jacks, the offer doesn't need to be substantial, only of value to your audience. Smart companies give great offers that leverage the discount to generate acquisition and drive up revenue.

Why don't we see more companies using the Cracker Jack strategy? Their offers are usually too hearty to begin with, and they end up taking a loss because the response was too grand. Or the offer was buried in text or was simply too difficult for the user to access. The sad story is 80% of website visitors will never return after their initial visit and that special opportunity is gone forever. Furthermore, the company, after feeling burned, will never indulge in this potent marketing technique again. Do it right the first time and watch that list grow.

Landing page testimonials
The testimonial is one of the last pieces I have seen on e-newsletter signup landing pages that really separate the good from the best at persuading a visitor to sign up to be on your e-mail list. Get those

satisfied customers to rave about you. Go one step further and record their audio and place them on your website. Your webmaster can easily and affordably help you. If you've been told it's expensive to have a 30-second audio testimonial on your site, then you ought to look for audio on the web assistance elsewhere. Of course, my company excels at adding the soundtrack to your website, but I would never try to promote that here.

(www.hartcreativemarketing.com)

Lastly, on the topic of testimonials and their misuse, don't replace your selling thrust with testimonials. Rather, use them to augment your thrust. Don't use the ones that read as if they were written by you. Use real ones, ones that are believable to your particular audience.

Testimonials may actually harm response if your target is top-level executives or leaders of any type. "Pioneers" are not often influenced by other people's opinions and may resent that kind of approach. If your prospects are "emulators," however, testimonials can be extremely effective.

10.   Your "From" Line: Benefit or Barrier?

> Who it is from tells them to read on (or not).

Over the years, I've seen many studies on the "from" line. Most results prove that 60% of respondents cite the "from" line as the most important factor motivating them to open e-mails, while 35% cited the "subject" line.

The "from" line is all about getting recipients past that first critical step to e-mail success: the open. How can you make sure your "from" line maximizes your open rate rather than creating a barrier to open? The following eight tips are guaranteed to help.

Your "from" line has two parts:

> **Part one** is the "From Name": the name, such as "Hart Creative Marketing."

> **Part two** is the "From Address": the electronic address, including "@" such as, "enewsletter@jerryhart.com."

Your recipients may see only the From Name or only the From Address or both, depending on their e-mail client or reader.

- **Be consistent.** Recipients will become familiar with your communications and look for your specific From Name and/or From Address in their e-mail inboxes. Consistency in your From Name and From Address will ensure that your e-mail is recognized and opened.

- **Become a trusted sender.** Encourage recipients to put your From Address in their address book, trusted sender list, or approved sender list (whatever the e-mail client may call it) to ensure that they receive the e-mail rather than having it sent to their spam or junk folder.

  - New anti-spam features in AOL and Outlook are designed to place spam control in the hands of recipients and to protect them from unwanted visual images. In some e-mail software, your beautiful HTML layout will appear, but images will not be visible unless you are on the recipient's trusted sender or contact list.

  - If you're a trusted sender or contact, your e-mail will be delivered and remain exempt from anti-spam measures, including filters, challenge response systems, or image blockers.

  - Make it easy for recipients to add your From Address to their trusted sender or contact list by keeping it short, easy to remember, and easy to type. Doing this will also make it easier for recipients to search for your previous e-mail newsletters and offers whenever they need to.

- **Make it meaningful.** Both your From Name and your From Address should identify you and/or your company as the sender of the e-mail and clarify the relationship between you and the recipient. Take this opportunity to give the recipient a reason to open your e-mail instead of a reason to delete it.

- **Use a From Name and From Address the recipient will recognize.** Recipients signed up to be on your list. They know your name, your product or service name, or your company name, and are expecting to hear from you.
- **Use your brand.** The "from" line is an important branding opportunity. As such, it is a good idea to use a From Name and/or From Address that includes your name, or the name of your company, product, or service, whichever the recipient will know best. Your brand in the "from" line assures the recipient that the e-mail is coming from a reliable and trusted source and builds familiarity and your credibility—especially when repeated over time.

- **Keep your "from" line short.** Doing this will ensure that your "from" line will appear in its entirety in the recipient's inbox. If the recipient's e-mail client displays both the From Name and From Address, things can get awfully cramped and even hidden. If there is some reason your From Name and From Address have to be long, at least make sure the most important identifier comes first, like so: "Hart Creative Marketing Expert" People know Jerry Hart in my community, but new readers don't know me, yet! Therefore, starting with Jerry Hart is very important to pass that five second "they may delete me if I'm not recognizable" test.

- **Avoid using a From Address like any of these:**
  - PayDayToday@luckydice.biz—Looks like a smarmy online gambling site. DELETE!
  - k3mm7u3vx901@hotmail.com—Hmmm, a bunch of random letters and numbers. DELETE!
  - youknowme@blast.net—Don't think so. DELETE!
  - getpaidfornothing@mx11.sleightoftheupperhand.com—You're kidding, right? DELETE!

- **Avoid using a From Name like any of these:**
  - The Answer—Could you be any more vague? DELETE!
  - Sexy Angie—Dime a dozen porn site. DELETE!
  - Size Matters—Gee, I wonder what this is? DELETE!
  - Prank Call—Could this actually be a prank E-mail follow-up? DELETE!

As you examine your "from" line and consider these tips, remember that there are pros and cons to change. You may already have a "from" line that works just great for you. You may have a sizable list of recipients who have already added your From Address to their trusted sender list, contact list, or address book. In that case, "If it ain't broke, don't fix it." However, if you are just starting out or see room for improvement in your "from" line, now may be the perfect time to make a change.

11. Classic E-Newsletter Mistakes

The twelve deadly e-newsletter mistakes you should avoid at all costs.

Confusing newsletters with promotions

Many marketers don't make the distinction between an e-mail newsletter and e-mail promotions. The latter are action-oriented, designed to provoke some kind of (immediate) response with a click-through, a signup, and a purchase—whatever. They're what most people think of under the term opt-in e-mail marketing.

E-newsletters may contain action-related elements, but their real potential is in building, over time, a lasting, long-term relationship with the reader, which means they may not try to induce any kind of immediate action at all. Instead, they create a climate, an environment, and a relationship, which predisposes the reader to taking such an action at some other time.

You can think of promotions as transaction-oriented and newsletters as relationship-oriented. An e-mail promotion says, "Buy the new Brownlow Desk Chair 2006," the e-mail newsletter carries an article about avoiding back strain in the office. If you don't get the difference clear in your head, then you're likely to commit the following two mistakes as well.

Being too publisher-centric
A successful newsletter delivers useful information, at the right time, and to the right people. With competition for inbox space growing, even that isn't always enough, though.

The reader is actually interested in information that addresses a problem or need (for help, humor, marketing intelligence, industry insight, etc.). If you can work your products and services into addressing those needs and problems, and avoid sounding like a promotion, fine. But you'll generally need to be more innovative than that. For example, share a universal symptom the audience relates to, then offer the solution to that specific symptom. It's a classic form of productization and a sure way to not appear like you're trying to sell.

Content
Good articles are fundamental to any good newsletter. The right content will be objective and targeted to your ideal reader. It'll fit their preferences and reading styles.

Make sure that the majority of your content isn't about you at all, but don't be afraid to be a little promotional (make sure to link the newsletter to what you do). Include testimonials, case studies, links to recent press, and sales or special promotions. For best results, consider outsourcing this crucial newsletter function to a professional newsletter writer.

Using the wrong success metrics
Calculating newsletter return on investment is a tough nut to crack, since newsletter costs are immediate and relatively easy to measure, while the benefits are long-term and difficult to measure.

One approach is to measure the revenue produced by subscribers before and after they subscribed, and compare this with a control group of nonsubscribers.

Nameplate

The nameplate (the area where your newsletter's name appears, sometimes mistaken for the masthead) should be consistent from issue to issue and should give both your newsletter's name and your company name.

For HTML newsletters, tie your nameplate to your company's image using the same colors, fonts, or a logo. All newsletters should work to establish a tie between each issue and your company.

Masthead

All e-mail newsletters should have contact information. Make it as easy as possible to contact you and don't force readers to visit your website to do so because they won't.

Make e-mail and website addresses clickable and maximize the masthead's impact by keeping it brief and consistent each issue. The masthead is a great place to include a brief section on what you do to familiarize prospects with your company.

Ignoring the value of the headers

You hear a lot about subject lines in e-mail marketing, but not a lot about the other e-mail headers, particularly the "to" and "from" headers.

Consider a newsletter which arrives thus:

From: server11@somenewsletterservice.com
To: list member e-mail address
Subject: Brownlow Chairs

Now compare it with this one:
From: mark.brownlow@brownlowchairs.com
To: Customer Name
Subject: [Brownlow Chairs] A desktop health and safety tip...

Use a combination of the three headers to:
- Maintain the impression that it's a one-to-one communication.

- Identify a recognizable sender (the relevant brand, person, website, or company).

- Identify the publication.

- Give recipients something they can use for filtering their e-mail (into a "chair newsletters" folder, for example) or encourage the recipients to open and read the mail.

Making it difficult for people to unsubscribe

Some marketers still believe a disgruntled subscriber is better than no subscriber at all. So they make people jump through hoops to get off an address list, or they wait a few more newsletter issues until the unsubscribe request is properly honored.

At best, the would-be ex-subscriber manages to get unsubscribed and leaves with a bad impression. At worst, he or she remains trapped in your distribution list. So you pay for e-mails to go unread, and suffer as the recipient complains to all and sundry about your poor administration, not to mention the spam accusations.

Trapped subscribers also lower response rates to any advertisements and other offers in your newsletter, skewing the statistics and disappointing any third-party advertisers. So make your unsubscribe process quick and painless.

Not making the most of website traffic or customers for signups

Obviously, the more targeted your subscribers, the better your results. That's why a list of 5000 subscribers can outperform one with 500,000.

Where do you look for these perfect subscribers? Clearly, you'll want to encourage website visitors to sign up, but please, only require their name and e-mail address. If you require any more personal information that they don't feel comfortable sharing with you, you might lose the chance to get just their name and e-mail address. Also, consider the places this audience spends time and post helpful solutions related to your newsletter on discussion boards (using a brief signature to promote the newsletter) and advertise at selected websites. By filling your list with targeted subscribers, you'll improve your results exponentially.

Think of the effort invested in persuading website visitors to become customers. Then compare this with the typical effort expended to persuade them to become newsletter subscribers. How many times have you seen a subscription box tagged on the bottom of a web page, with no indication of the newsletter's contents, frequency, privacy policies, etc.?

Give people the opportunity to sign up for a newsletter everywhere: web pages, confirmation messages, thank you pages, receipts, etc. At the least, let people know what will happen when they submit their address, what they can expect in their
e-mail inboxes and how often they can expect it, and what you'll do or won't do with their e-mail address. (This means posting a prominent privacy policy.)

Tagline

All newsletters should have a sentence that describes the newsletter's subject and audience. A line like, "Basic basket weaving for kids," tells potential subscribers at a glance whether or not your newsletter's what they're looking for.

A good tagline will identify the audience, the subject matter, and the benefits. The tagline appears near the nameplate or in the masthead and can also be used as your e-mail signature. It should be brief yet memorable. Save the sales pitch for something else because the last thing you want is for potential readers to think the newsletter's "salesy."

Distribution

From personalization, to the sender's name, e-mail distribution requires making choices. Consider using a distribution service that allows the reader's name to be added to the subject line and body. Also, if you're using HTML, will you have two separate lists, or will you use multipart MIME?

Set up the to and from fields so the newsletter comes from the editor and goes specifically to one reader's e-mail address. Of all the newsletter issues, distribution can easily become the most complicated; so don't just select the first provider you find.

Some great choices include: Cooler E-mail, Constant Contact, Hart Creative Marketing, Inc.

Ask

In each issue, make sure you ask your readers for action, whether you want them to call and set up a consultation or place an order. You'll need to ask to get real results.

A newsletter that delivers business isn't far off if you round up the usual suspects. Take care to establish a firm foundation, ask for what you want, and get ready to record the results. In no time, your newsletter will be one that attracts customers, builds loyalty, and increases profits.

Checklists

What news can you offer your customers that will keep them asking for more?

_____

_____

_____

_____

_____

_____

List your audience segments.

_____

_____

_____

Take 1 or 2 segments from you list above and determine your ideal customer profile.

_____

_____

_____

_____

_____

Locate 5 newsletters you like and describe why you like them?

_____

_____

_____

_____

Find 3 to 5 newsletters you dislike and describe why you do not like them.

_____

_____

_____

_____

_____

_____

Out of the items from the above two questions, list the items you would like to see in your own newsletter.

_____

_____

_____

_____

_____

_____

_____

How often do you plan on publishing your newsletter? Can you commit to being on schedule and on time?

_____

_____

Would you buy products from the information in your newsletter?
Why or why not?

_____

_____

_____

_____

_____

What topics for your newsletter do you plan to use for the next 4
months?

_____

_____

_____

_____

_____

List 8 to 10 places you can find subscribers for your email list.

_____

_____

_____

_____

_____

_____

_____

_____

_____

_____

8.   Search Engines, Part I

1.   The Main Search Engines

List yourself everywhere but do it correctly.

We could write a long list of search engines with descriptions of each, but what really matters is simple: If you are targeting the U.S. market, you have to be on Google (about 65% of all searches are done on Google or Google-powered search engines), Yahoo (about 15%), and MSN (about 15%). The remaining 5% doesn't matter.

- You also need to be in the directories. Because the directories are built and edited by humans, they are considered reliable. The contents of directories are used by many search engines for their indexes. The two main directories are Yahoo! and DMOZ.

- There are also specialty search engines. If your market is large enough that there is a portal or search engine for it, then investigate those search engines and learn how to get your site listed.

- There's also automated submission. "Pay $10 and have your website submitted to 600 Search Engines!" You don't have to submit your website at all. If your website has good information, others in your cluster will link to your website and the search engines will find you.

Search Engine Spamming

You've heard of e-mail spamming, now we also have Search Engine Spamming. E-mail spam is unsolicited content sent to one's e-mail inbox without the recipient's consent to do so. Spamming a Search Engine is as much a crime as e-mail spamming. Here's what you want to avoid doing to ensure the search engines never think of shutting you down from search visibility.

I admit, I did this one, then had to remove the text I was hiding on my home page by making it the same color as the background color on the site.

Don't use the same keywords in great numbers anywhere in your site, in the code in the back, out front inside the HTML, or on any page using text or design images.

2. The Goal of Search Engines

How do you rank?

There are some six billion webpages (as of spring 2005), but only a third of these are indexed. The rest are ignored. Search engines don't index abandoned pages or trivial pages. How do the search engines know if a page is trivial? They check to see if other pages link to it. If the page has low informational value, other people won't bother to link to it. There are some two billion trivial webpages, which is about a third of the web. Search engines also ignore duplicate pages, redirects (pages that jump to other pages), and obsolete or abandoned pages. These make up another third of the web.

This leaves some two billion pages. Search engines use various strategies to index and rank those pages:

- Categorize the web into collections of information clusters. For example, all the pages about Macintosh computers form a cluster. Pages about the Berlin Wall form another cluster.

- Place webpages within those clusters according to their informational value (the quality of the information), links to the webpage within the cluster, and other criteria.

- Downplay, ignore, or ban irrelevant webpages or webpages that manipulate search engines.

In the beginning, Yahoo! indexed the web manually. They had rooms full of humans who indexed webpages. However, as the web grew explosively, they couldn't keep up, so automated indexing tools began to be developed for search engines. These use various rules to automatically sort webpages into categories and then rank those pages according to significance. This works fairly well, but new problems arise from the nature of the technologies.

3. The Mathematical Nature of the Web

What percentage of your web traffic goes to the first page compared to the second page?

To understand ranking, we have to look at how items are listed in the search engine results. You search for a topic and the search engine returns a list of webpages. What does it mean to be on the fifth page in comparison to the tenth page? What percentage of traffic goes to the first page compared to the second page? Is there a way to calculate this?

In daily life, numbers are linear: they grow according to simple addition. You drive your car at 40 mph. If you increase the speed to 50 mph, that's 10 mph faster. To understand car speeds, you only need to add or subtract numbers.

Logarithms are another kind of number. In California, we're quite familiar with log numbers. Earthquakes are measured by the Richter Scale, which is based on logarithmic numbers. A Richter 5.0 is ten times more powerful than a Richter 4.0. A Richter 6.0 is ten times more powerful than a 5.0 and 100 times more powerful than a 4.0.

By the mid 1990s, physics researchers began to study the web. They quickly discovered that the growth, quantity, and distribution of links on the web are based on log numbers. For example, say your webpage is on the third page at Google. If we look at three as a logarithmic number, then page one gets basically 90% of the traffic for that topic, page two gets a tenth of the traffic, and page three gets 1% of the traffic. If a webpage isn't on the first three pages in a search engine, that's pretty much the same as not being there at all.

If people apply linear numbers to the web, they will seriously misunderstand what is happening. They will think that going from the page two hundred to page five is a great improvement. However, seen from a log scale, that is hardly any difference. If we put these numbers on a linear graph, they make little sense. The line creeps along at the bottom of the graph and then suddenly spikes off the chart.

In a Consumers Union study, 88% of users stayed on the first page of the search engine results, 16% went on to the second page, but only 2% went as far as the third page. In a study by Excite.com of one million searches by 200,000 users, it was found that 70% looked at only the first two pages of results. Another study found 97% of users clicked only the first ten links and 71% of those clicked only the first five links. In a University of Pennsylvania study, 50% of users viewed only the first page of results, 19% went to the second page, and 10% went to the third page; 55% of users looked at only the first item while 80% looked at only the first three items. As you can guess, those numbers are logarithmic distributions.

> A few webpages have lots of traffic. The vast majority of webpages get little traffic. There is no gradual transition or equal distribution. You get either nearly all the traffic in your category or you get crumbs. Logarithmic distribution applies to personal webpages, corporate webpages, university webpages, and the web as a whole. It also applies to the distribution of keywords. A few keywords will get most of the traffic.

Google uses an algorithm (a mathematical formula) to rank the webpages in its index. The Google algorithm's main idea is simple: pages are ranked by the number of links to those pages. The more links to a page, the more valuable that page is. A link to a page is a vote for that page. Someone else thought the page was significant and so added a link to it.

However, this method also has nonobvious implications. If people vote for webpages, it seems that doing so would rank the pages fairly evenly. The good ones would be at the top, most would be in the middle, and the bad ones end up at the bottom. However, it doesn't happen that way because the web's distribution is based on logarithms. The result is that a few pages get a disproportionate amount of the votes and most pages get very little. Thus, the Google algorithm uses logarithms to rank webpages.

Webpages can also be classified by the type of links they have. The IBM Almaden Research Center in Silicon Valley studied the link distribution in a small collection of two hundred million webpages and found that the web consists of five groups:

- 28% of webpages are the core of the web. These pages are highly crosslinked among other core webpages.
- 21% of webpages lead into the core. These pages point to the core, but there are no links from the core to these pages.
- 21% of webpages are linked from the core. The core links to these pages, but the pages have no links to the core or other pages.
- 22% of webpages form a number of groups that are linked from the core, but these groups don't lead to other groups or to the core.
- 8% of webpages are isolated islands. There are no links to or from these pages.

So, why are there so many isolated webpages or pages without links to other pages? Many companies refuse to crosslink their sites. They want to trap the visitors within their site. A link allows the visitor to go away. However, this means that other sites probably won't link to these pages and they will have less traffic.

4. *The Network*

> What does it mean when people say
> the web is a network?

Let's look at the field of network theory in mathematics and physics. By understanding this theory, you'll know how the web grows, why the top websites grow yet faster, and how a few websites can affect the rest of the websites within their cluster.

In the 1730s, Leonhard Euler, a Swiss mathematician and physicist, invented the field of network theory, and for most of the next two hundred years it was a form of abstract mathematics. A network is made up of nodes and links. Nodes are the connectors and links are the connections between nodes. For example, in a social network, nodes are the people and links are the friendships between them. On the web, nodes are the webpages and links are the links between webpages.

In network theory, mathematicians assumed the links between the nodes were randomly distributed. If there are, say, 10 nodes and 50 links, they assumed each node had on average five links.

If one applies the random distribution of networks to the social world, then six billion humans (the nodes) should each have generally the same number of friendships (the links). However, sociologists and economists realized that real-world networks were not randomly distributed.

In the early 1900s, Vilfredo Pareto, an Italian economist, discovered the 80/20 Rule, which says 20% of landowners own 80% of the land, 20% of salespeople make 80% of sales, and so on; and we can add, 20% of webpages get 80% of the traffic.

Stanley Milgram performed his famous six-degrees-of-separation experiment in the 1960s. The popular understanding of Milgram's experiment is that anyone can be linked to anyone else on Earth through only six links. In fact, Milgram discovered:

Three links of separation: Some people have such good links that they can get to someone far away through only three links.

One hundred links of separation: Others require up to a hundred links to reach someone else. This also means the people within those hundred links are also poorly linked.

No links: Milgram also found that many people have such poor links that they can't establish a connection to distant others. These people live in small social networks, but they are isolated from society at large.

In the late 1960s, sociologist Mark Granovetter studied how people found jobs. Until then, it was generally assumed that society was homogeneous and everyone had pretty much the same access as everyone else. Granovetter discovered that society is made up of *groups* of people, which is now known as clustering. Granovetter showed that weak contacts were twice as effective (28%) as strong contacts (17%) for finding a job. Casual connections were more likely to lead to a job.

This seems counterintuitive. It would seem close friends would be better job leads. However, we tend to gather within groups of similar interests. Sociologists call this the "birds of a feather" phenomenon, as in "birds of a feather flock together." For example, if a tennis instructor wants new students, there's no point for her to ask her friends because they are all tennis instructors. She will find new students by asking people in social clusters outside of tennis, such as church groups, knitting clubs, and so on. Those social clusters probably lack members who are tennis instructors.

These various sociological phenomena were known, but there was no satisfactory explanation for them because there was no way to quantify large social networks. You can write down a list of your friends, but this will grow very fast when you add the list of friends of friends. If you add a further circle of friends of friends of friends, the numbers become too large. What was needed was a real-world network that could be exhaustively mapped, such as the web.

5. The Internet as a Network

What is a link?

In the mid-1990s, physicists began studying the web because it was an example of a network in which all the nodes and links could be tracked. Although the internet was originally designed to be randomly distributed, computer scientists realized there was a pattern to its distribution. Maps of the web showed that some nodes had huge numbers of links, while most nodes had only a few links.

Albert-Lazlo Barabasi, a physics researcher, discovered that computer networks use logarithmic distribution, highly linked nodes grow faster, and networks undergo phase transitions. The distribution of links in a network can be measured by logarithmic numbers. A few nodes get most of the links. Most nodes have few links.

As new nodes enter the network, they are more likely to link to highly linked nodes than to low-link nodes because the highly linked nodes are easier to reach. This creates a feedback loop in which the largest nodes get larger. (The rich get richer.) Barabasi calls this "preferential linking."

Networks undergo phase transition. When a tipping point is crossed, all of the nodes undergo a phase transition and start acting as a single entity. This means the property of the network is shared among all nodes in the network. For example, when you heat water, the temperature slowly increases. But at some point, all of the water suddenly begins to boil. There is no gradual boiling or localized boiling.

In terms of websites, logarithmic distribution means that a few websites will get the majority of the market. Due to preferential linking, the largest sites will grow yet larger. As for phase transition, there can be a number of dotcoms in a small market and at first the various websites will be different. But when the market niche reaches a certain size, a few of the websites become very large and the remainder stay small. All of the websites take on the properties of the group. In other words, the small websites adapt the general standards of the largest websites.

Incidentally, this also shows why networks (the web, social networks, biological networks, and so on) easily survive attacks. If a computer virus spreads into a network and destroys perhaps 10% of all nodes, that's not really a problem, because 80% of nodes have low value. Losing many low-value nodes will not affect the network as a whole. However, if an attack targets the key nodes (the 20%), the result can be catastrophic. The entire network may collapse.

6. *How Search Engines Rank Websites*

Are all search engines created equally?

Yahoo!, one of the first web directories, was started by two Stanford postgraduate students, Jerry Yang and David Filo, in their dorm room as a list of websites that was maintained manually. If you wanted to be added to Yahoo!, you sent a personal e-mail to them and they would index your website in their directory. That worked for the first year or so, when there were only several thousand websites.

However, the web soon began to grow to several million pages and the two students had to hire workers to continue adding sites, but soon it became obvious that the web was growing too fast to keep up and the web would soon be too large to be maintained manually by humans.

Search engines needed a way to automate the indexing and ranking of the web. This meant a computer program was needed that could do this on its own. A similar problem had occurred in the early 1900s. Scientific journals were growing in number faster than the ability of librarians to index them. So, in the 1920s, researchers conducted research in library science on how to evaluate articles and journals. In the early 1960s, one researcher, Derek John de Solla Price, published two books that introduced modern bibliometrics.

The first citation analysis was carried out in 1926 by a husband and wife team, P. L. K. Gross and E. M. Gross, who examined 3,633 citations in the 1926 volume of the *Journal of the American Chemical Society*. They noticed that articles in chemistry journals had citations to other articles. If an article were significant, other researchers would cite it in their research. If it were not significant, it would have few citations. This meant it was possible to create a system so that nonchemists could assign the significance of an article simply by counting how many other articles cited it.

In the mid 1990s, Sergey Brin and Lawrence Page, two computer science researchers at Stanford, wrote a computer program that used bibliometrics to analyze the value of webpages. Just as with chemistry journal articles, the Brin and Page method ranked a webpage by the number of other pages that linked to it. If a page were significant, other people would take the effort to create a link to it. If the page were trivial, there would be few or no links to it.

Brin and Page's software became known as Google. While it's not the only links analysis tool, and it's not necessarily the best one, it is one of the best-known examples of computerized bibliometrics, which is also known as cybermetrics. Google's method assigns an authority value to a page. If many pages link to it, the target page is an authority. Jon Kleinberg, a researcher with IBM, proposed that a page should have an authority value (how many pages link to it) and a hub value (how many pages it points to.) Another version of Kleinberg's algorithm ranks a webpage if it points to major authorities. If your webpage lists the five top magazines and the international and national associations in your business, then the webpage has informational value.

These various tools can be tested by using the same dataset, making a search, and comparing the results. Link analysis works well when the topic is clearly defined, there are significant articles about it, and it has an interconnected community of webpages. But if these criteria aren't met, several odd problems can occur. For example, if a group of pages are highly interlinked within a tight-knit community, the pages can appear to be significant because they have many links although they have no real value. For example, several years ago a bunch of bloggers linked the words "dismal failure" to George W. Bush's personal page at the White House. If you search for dismal failure, you got George W. Bush.

If the topic is vague, or there aren't good webpages about it, or there aren't interconnected communities that discuss the issue, then the search engines produce wrong results. This is known as the topic drift problem. For example, search for "net gain." This produces 6.8 million hits, but the results are random pages.

You can see the implications of network theory for your webpage. Companies that pursue a "business is war" strategy are at a self-inflicted disadvantage. They create few links, newcomers don't link to them, their websites are isolated, and so on.

Companies that embed themselves into their information cluster by creating lots of links to other companies, suppliers, industry magazines, customers, government, and workers will grow, because the node with the most links will get more links. At some point, the network will undergo a phase transition from "just a bunch of separate companies" into an industry. The core companies become institutionalized and they own the industry. Their internal standards become the industry's standard. Pareto's 80/20 Rule applies and 20% of the companies will get 80% of the revenues. Due to the law of preferential linking, newcomers will be effectively locked out of the market space.

Information Clusters

The search engines identify clusters of information on the web, such as the cluster for cars, the cluster for government, and so on. Search engines then place webpages into those clusters. Webpages featuring information about the Porsche are placed in the cars cluster and so on. Look at your website's key idea. What is your website about? Search for that general keyword at Google and Yahoo! to find the cluster your webpage should fit into. Study the top-ranking pages in that cluster and then create your webpage (or restructure your website) to match that cluster.

Google will tell you your webpage's category. For example, search Google for koi. Click the More button and then click Directory. Search for koi once again. In the new results window, at the top, Google lists the category.

The category will be stated at the top and for each entry. For the first entry, the category is Recreation>Pets>Fish and Aquariums>Freshwater>Species>Koi. For the second entry, the category is Recreation>Pets>Fish and Aquaria>Clubs>North America>United States.

After the search engine places your webpage within a cluster, it ranks your page's value in that cluster. Google does this by looking at the number of links to your page from the cluster. If there are lots of links to your page, people in that cluster consider your page to be valuable. If there are few links, your page has low value.

So, how do you get other pages to link to you? Provide great information at your website and people will link to you on their own. If you write a useful article about how to cure fungus on a koi, dozens of koi owners, aquarium stores, and koi magazines will link to you.

Clusters and incoming links are among the most important concepts in this chapter. Create a webpage that is clearly focused on your cluster and add great content that is available for free. If you do only these two, you'll have great search engine optimization (SEO).The search engines will categorize you in the appropriate cluster, other pages will link to you, and your page will be ranked high.

You can also get people from related categories to link to you. For your koi website, try to get links from other animal and pet websites, such as for cats, dogs, veterinarians, gardening, yard landscaping, and so on.

However, links are not equal. Google ranks a webpage by the quality of the links that point to it. The quality of those links is the logarithmic value of each webpage (the Google PageRank value). But there's a further complication: the final value depends on the PageRank value of the page divided by the number of links on that page.

- For example, the New York Times has a PageRank 8. The Times publishes an article about your webpage and includes a link to your webpage. This means you get points for having a PageRank 8 page linked to you. However, the final value will be the PageRank divided by the number of links in the article. If the New York Times has a list of 10 links, the PageRank 8 divided by 10 is 0.8 points.

- The Montana Koi Ranchers Quarterly has a PageRank 4. It publishes an article about your webpage, and the link to your page is the only one in the story. The value to your page will be PageRank 4 divided by one, 4.

This means a small article in Montana can give you more points than a big article in the New York Times. It's better to be linked at a page with few links than a page with many links. Ideally, an incoming page should have a few hundred words of text and one link with a relevant keyword that points to your webpage.

By ranking webpages according to the number of incoming links, Google makes it very difficult for spammers to twist the results, since it's hard to get hundreds of sites to link to you.

- Don't turn away pages with a low PageRank. Your webpage's PageRank is a total of all pages that link to you. Even small webpages will give you a few points. Dozens of low PageRank pages will give you a higher cumulative result than a few high PageRank pages. Furthermore, if your PageRank depends on only a few large PageRank pages and one of them removes the link to your page, your PageRank will be affected dramatically. With lots of low PageRank pages, the loss of a few links will have little effect on your overall PageRank.

- Before you link to a website, check its PageRank. If it has PageRank of 0 and it has been around for a while, that means Google has blacklisted it. If you link to a "bad neighborhood," you will be penalized. If a bad page links to you, you won't lose points. Google penalizes you only for what is under your control.

There are strategies for creating the links within your website. If you crosslink every page to every other, all of your pages will have a low PageRank because the value is averaged out across all pages. Instead, you can direct the PageRank value to the most important pages. Add links from the main pages to the minor pages. The minor pages should have links with appropriate keywords to (and only to) the main pages. The minor pages should not crosslink with each other. This focuses the PageRank value on the main pages.

If you have good free information at your website, let other websites know about it. Send a summary and a link in an e-mail to the websites within your cluster that have a higher PageRank than your website. Include your main keywords in the link text.

7. *Keywords*

> Not everyone can spell, take advantage of it.

A major step in search engine optimization is to develop the list of keywords that are relevant to your website. Also, think about phrases, not just words. Most users use two or more keywords when they search. Instead of just koi, add the words Japanese koi fish, koi goldfish pool, koi ornamental pond, and so on.

Don't forget about misspellings. Adding misspelled versions of the keyword, such as "goldfish" will help you: search for "goldfsih" and you'll see how many others have misspelled it. Also, delete irrelevant keywords. Search engines will penalize your site if it has unrelated keywords. For example, if your site is in the koi cluster yet you have keywords such as Britney Spears, the search engines may consider that as a form of spoofing.

If your site is regional, add regional keywords, such as names of your province, city, valley, and so on. For example, Chicago Koi, Happy Valley Koi, or Tennessee Koi. You can also use regional variants and slang. Say you're selling crawfish— these are also called crayfish, crawdads, craw daddy, mud bugs, and so on. Use an unabridged dictionary or regional dictionaries to find these words.

If your website has an international market, then translate the keywords. However, you can't simply convert your keywords from one language into another. For example, house and home are different words in English, but only one word in Spanish. There are plenty of examples of inadvertently funny translated slogans. You should work with a translator who understands marketing in that language.

The value of an incoming link is based on a combination of the inbound page's PageRank value and the keywords in that page's link. A page that has lots of keywords and a good PageRank value will rank higher in Google than a page that has a higher PageRank value. For example, search for koi and you'll find the first page is vcnet.com (PageRank 5), the second is coloradokoi.com (PageRank 4), and the sixth site is akca.org (PageRank 6). The highest ranking page (PageRank 6) is ranked lower than the others. Although akca.org has a higher PageRank, Google calculates that for this search (koi), the other sites are more relevant.

Now, use your keywords to write your sales pitch. This should be a short sentence that uses the top two or three keywords and describes your site's purpose and your product or service. Use a short sentence that your grandmother will understand. "Empowering agents to dynamically access the vertical market" doesn't say anything. Use complete sentences. Google prefers keywords within a sentence because a sentence has more information.

- The best sales pitch is a spoken phrase, not a written sentence. Try saying the sales pitch to your friends and co-workers. It's good when it doesn't sound awkward. To get ideas for your sales pitch, study your top competitors. They probably have written sales pitches for their websites. Read the Google AdWords results for your keyword and look at their websites.

The sales pitch should be more than a short statement such as "We sell koi." It should contain your top two or three keywords, names of specific products or services, and, if relevant, your location. It should also be personal. For example: "Koi-Heaven.com is your wholesale distributor of kohaku, showa, and asagi koi in Chicago."

8.   URL, Title Tag, Meta-Description

If you are worried about how many different

Use your main keyword to create the website's URL. Search engines look at the words in the URL. Koi-Heaven.com is going to rank higher than LarryAndJane.com when you search for koi.

Always use a hyphen and not an underscore in your URL. For example, use koi-heaven, not koi_heaven. Google treats the hyphen as a space and the underscore as a character. This means that koi-heaven will be found if someone searches for koi, heaven, or koi heaven, but koi_heaven will be found only if someone searches for koi_heaven.

- Put your main keyword at the beginning of the URL. Koi-Heaven.com is better than Heaven-for-Koi.com. If you already have a URL such as LarryAndJane.com that doesn't match your keyword, then consider changing your current URL. You can set up a redirect on the old site to point to the new site.

The title tag is in the HTML's HEAD section. The code looks like this:
<TITLE>Koi and Goldfish at Koi-Heaven.com</TITLE>

The title is displayed in the upper left of the browser window. Here's an example of a title tag.

The title is also used in the description text that appears in the search engine.

Here's a sampling of titles from Google:

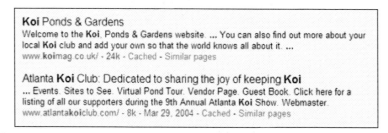

The title tag's content is what the user sees in the search engine results list.

- Write a good title that will encourage visitors to come to your website.

- When writing the title, use the keyword first and then the name of the website—for example, Koi and ornamental goldfish at Koi-Heaven.com.

- Search engines limit the number of characters that they will read from the title tag. The number varies according to the search engine, but as a rule use no more than 50 characters, including spaces.

The meta-description tag also goes in the HEAD section. Here's an example:

<meta name="Description" content="A beginner's guide to keeping koi fish in a backyard pond.">

Search engines display the content of the description tag to the visitor in the search engine results page. Let's look again at those results. Google fetches the content for the two lines of descriptive text from the webpage's meta-description tag. In the following examples, the first two descriptions are sentences but the third is sentence fragments:

Koi Carp and Fish Ponds Information
A beginner's guide to keeping **Koi** fish in a backyard recirculated freshwater pond. A Beginners Guide to **Koi** and **Koi** Ponds. Introduction ...
www.vcnet.com/koi_net/ - 4k - Cached - Similar pages

KOI USA Magazine - The magazine for all koi enthusiasts
KOI USA Magazine The magazine for all **koi** enthusiasts. A ... events. KOI USA Magazine is 140 jam-packed pages in bright, full color. ...
www.koiusa.com/ - 23k - Mar 24, 2004 - Cached - Similar pages

KoiVet.com - Koi and Golfish Health Care
KoiVet.com - **Koi** and Goldfish Health Care, KoiVet.com - **Koi** and Goldfish Health Care, ... Want **Koi** News? **Koi** News as it happens, with an archive to boot! ...
www.koivet.com/ - 57k - Mar 24, 2004 - Cached - Similar pages

---

The third item has a number of ellipses. This means that Google isn't using the description tag. Either there isn't a meta-description tag or for some reason Google chose to ignore it. Instead, Google's software is fetching text from the body of the webpage. It ignores superlative marketing text, such as "We're the best in the world!" and instead shows sentence fragments that indicate information (such as archive, news, health care, and so on.)

To write your description tag,

- Use your top two or three keywords and write a complete sentence.

- Look at other descriptions in Google and notice what they consider important, such as the words archive, news, health care, and similar.

- Put the keyword first, then the description, and finally the company name. "Keep beautiful Koi and goldfish in your pond. News, FAQ, tips, information, and more at Koi-Heaven.com."

- Use about 250 characters.

- Include your telephone number or location/city/province in the description. Often, people will simply pick up the phone and call. For example: "Keep beautiful Koi and goldfish in your pond. News, FAQ, tips, information, and more at Koi-Heaven.com in Chicago. Call us at 800-KOI-FISH."

Here's how your webpage will appear in the Google listing:

Koi and Goldfish at Koi-Heaven.com
Keep beautiful Japanese **Koi** and goldfish in your pond. News, FAQ, tips, information, and more at Koi-Heaven.com in Chicago. Call us at 800-KOI-FISH.
www.koi-heaven.com/ - 23k - Mar 29, 2004 - Cached - Similar pages

9.   Submit Your Directory Descriptions

Descriptions are an important, make sure you are listed everywhere.

Now that you have the description, submit it to the Yahoo! and DMOZ directories. These lists are edited and maintained by humans. If they think your entry is valuable, they will add it to their directories. But remember to submit it as early as possible. Both of these directories can take months to add your site to their lists.

These directories are used by other search engines. The DMOZ file is open source and any search engine can fetch it for free and use it to create its list of webpages.

Since the DMOZ list is edited and evaluated by humans who are experts in those categories, it is considered to be more valuable than lists created by automated indexing tools.

- To submit to DMOZ, visit http://dmoz.org/add.html

- To submit to Yahoo!, visit:
http://search.yahoo.com/info/submit.html

The meta-keyword tag probably causes the most problems for those in Search Engine Optimization. The meta-keyword tag tells the search engine what the webpage's main keywords are.

Here's an example of a meta-keyword tag:
<meta name="keyword" content="koi, goldfish, fish, ponds, Japanese ornamental fish">

Lots of people have heard about this tag, and yes, it was once important, so they insist that those in Search Engine Optimization include this tag. However, nearly all of the major search engines ignore the meta-keyword tag because it's too easy to use this to fool the search engines.

There's also another problem with the meta-keyword tag: it tells your competitors what your keywords are. You put all this work into creating the ideal list of keywords and you then place that list in the meta-keyword field. JoesGunsAndKoi.com comes along, copies your list, and saves himself an afternoon of work.

Clients always ask us to add the meta-keyword tag. If I tell them it is useless, they think, "Ha! I saw this tip on Fox News! You don't know anything about SEO!"

So when clients want a meta-keyword tag, we put one in. It's just a few general keywords that don't give away the farm.

And of course, you can look at your competitors' sites and copy their meta-keyword tag into your list of keywords. Meta-keyword tags are still used in many intranet search engines. Persons within an organization are unlikely to spoof their own organization's search engine.

File names

The search engines index the names of files that make up your website. If one file is named koi-information.html and another is su-inf.html, you can guess which one will be found when a user searches for koi.

- Use your keywords for your file names; for example, koi-information.html, koi-fungus.html, and so on.

- Use informative names for your files. Avoid cryptic names, acronyms, and so on.

Directory names

The search engines index the text in the folder names. You can use the folder names to increase your keyword exposure to the search engines. If koi food is one of your keywords, then create a directory with that keyword. For example, Koi-Heaven.com/koi-food/koi-food.html.

The H1 header

Okay, now we're getting into the body of the HTML. Here is perhaps the most common search engine optimization error. Use an H1 heading on the front page. Google gives emphasis to words in the heading because headings carry information about a page. Web designers don't like the H1 heading because it's big and ugly. Instead of H1, they use images or body text and modify it with SPAN, DIV, or CSS. That looks nice, but Google wants to see a headline.

By using images or SPAN, the web designer inadvertently undermines the webpage's indexability. Images can't be indexed, so Google won't see those headings. Header text that uses SPAN will be treated as body text, not header text. To get Google to index the heading, use an H1 tag to mark the heading. Use the main keyword as the first word in the heading, such as Koi Experts of Chicago.

The body paragraph

The body text is the text on the front page. This text should be descriptive, informational, and have lots of keywords.

- Put your main keyword at the beginning of the body text.

- Repeat the main keyword several times within the first 25 words.

- Work the other keywords into the body text.

- Repeat the main keyword at the end of the front page.

- Use complete sentences in your text.

- Avoid phrases such as "Best in the World!" Some search engines ignore these kinds of phrases.

- Use words that mark information, such as news, guide, and summary.

- Google also offers Local Results. If a user adds a city name to a search, she will see a list of relevant businesses and services in her city. If your location is relevant to your product or service, add your city, telephone number, and zip code to your front page.

Checklists

Test your ranking in good by entering your keywords one at a time (are you located on the first three pages?)

_____

_____

_____

List your keywords and give the Google ranking for each.

_____

_____

_____

_____

_____

_____

_____

List all of your links to other websites. For each link determine their page rank. Include links you would like to have in the list.

_____

_____

_____

_____

_____

_____

_____

_____

Write a description tag for your website.

_____

_____

_____

_____

_____

_____

_____

_____

_____

NOTES

9.   Search Engines, Part II

1.　*More Effort to Get Attention*

> **How much text do you have in your hyperlinks?**

Search engines give more attention to the text in hyperlinks, since hyperlinks take effort to create and often point to information. Put the keywords in the hyperlink. Example: Read <a href=http://www.koi-heaven.com/koi-fungus.html>how to cure fungus in koi</a>. On the first page, add links that point to your informational pages. Note that the file has an informative and relevant file name.

What about site maps? Some websites use JavaScript or roll-down menus for the navigation. However, some search engines ignore JavaScript and thus won't follow the links at your site. Site maps that use images present the same problem. Create a plain text site map that lists all of the webpages. Place a plain text link to the site map on the index page.

Validate the HTML with validation software. Some search engines pay attention to the quality of your HTML. One difference between amateur and professional websites is whether the HTML is written correctly.

- Write clean HTML code. Use HTML validation software to make sure your code is compliant with the current standards

Remember the two billion webpages that are ignored because they've been abandoned? If you don't make occasional changes to your website, the search engines may conclude it is no longer active. Every few weeks, add a news item, a review, or a new item to your website. Update the front page. The search engines will give you a higher ranking. Google will also index your website more frequently if you get a higher ranking.

If you're wondering how to tell when Google has indexed your site, there's a way to find out. If Google has recently indexed your site, it adds the date of indexing to the results page. These are called fresh tags. In the following illustration, which was created in early April 2004, we see that Google indexed the second webpage on March 29th, 2004.

Koi Ponds & Gardens
Welcome to the **Koi**, Ponds & Gardens website. ... You can also find out more about your local **Koi** club and add your own so that the world knows all about it. ...
www.koimag.co.uk/ - 24k - Cached - Similar pages

Atlanta **Koi** Club: Dedicated to sharing the joy of keeping **Koi**
... Events. Sites to See. Virtual Pond Tour. Vendor Page. Guest Book. Click here for a listing of all our supporters during the 9th Annual Atlanta **Koi** Show. Webmaster.
www.atlantakoiclub.com/ - 8k - Mar 29, 2004 - Cached - Similar pages

Google indexes the web generally in the last week of the month. Webpages with high Google PageRank are indexed more frequently. If you have changes, be sure to add them by the 20th of the month so they'll be indexed.

Add blogs to your website. Blogs are a great way to quickly add content to your site. Just open a text box, type your entry, click submit, and you're done. If you want a free, quick-and-easy blog, then use blogger.com. If you want a better blog, you'll need one of the commercial blog tools. We've tested all of them; the best is movabletype.org.

2. Web Traffic Analysis

Your website keeps track of every action.

Your website keeps track of every action. All of this information is recorded in web traffic logs. You use log analysis programs to display this information in charts and tables. Traffic analysis lets you see:

- Which pages are popular or not. This tells you where to invest more effort, or which pages to delete.

- How users came to your site. It will list where the pages came from. You can contact those websites and suggest link exchanges.

- The websites that your visitors are hopping to. Again, you can contact those sites and suggest link exchanges.

- Which search engines are sending traffic to your website. You can increase your efforts at those search engines and reduce expenses at ineffective search engines.

- The keywords that users use when they search for your site. You can add those words to your keyword collection and develop additional material. You can delete ineffective words.

- In some cases, you may not want a search engine to index your webpage. Perhaps you have pages that are not relevant to the public. There are two ways to keep search engines out of your site: the robots.txt file and the robots meta tag.

- The robots.txt file lists files that should not be indexed by a search engine. Create a text file, add a list of files, save it as robots.txt, and place the file in the main HTML directory where your index file resides. However, just because you use this doesn't mean the page won't be indexed. There are hundreds of search engines and not all of them follow this protocol.

3.   *Flash, Graphics, Frames, and MORE*

Flash, graphics, frames, passwords, and broken links all have an effect.

Web designers and graphics designers love Flash, because it allows them to create beautiful websites. However, search engines cannot index Flash. The site looks great, but it will not be listed in search engines. Don't create a website that uses only images. Some designers do this to use unique fonts. It looks nice, but search engines can't read images and won't index them.

Websites from the mid-90s use frames. Many search engines can't index the content of frames. If your website uses frames, rebuild it so it does not. Pages behind a password will not be indexed. If there is content that you want to have indexed, then copy it to a nonsecured page. If a link is broken, the search engine can't follow it. Use link validation software to test the links.

Spammer techniques are rampant. Search engines use tools to look for these tricks and will blacklist your website if they find them. Link farms are pages that have dozens or hundreds of links. Spammer sites use these to bury their links among hundreds of valid links. Avoid link farms.

- Spammers use Meta-Refresh to misdirect visitors. You search for Britney Spears and go to a website named AllAboutBritneySpears.com where you realize in shock that you been redirected to a website about Justin Timberlake. This is done by using an instant refresh. Search engines will penalize for instant refresh. If you use meta-refresh tags, set the delay to five seconds or more.

- Cloaking and stealth scripts are used to mislead the search engines. The search engine is shown one website (all about Britney Spears) but the visitor is shown a different website (Justin Timberlake).

There are more spammer tricks, such as duplicate pages, keyword stuffing, fake pages that are not related to the website's real content, and keywords hidden with background colors. Don't use these or you'll be blacklisted.

So how do search engines deal with spammers? If a website is using spammer tricks, the website's ranking will be lowered or the website, including the IP address, will be blacklisted.

If one of your competitors is using spammer tricks, report them to the search engine to have them removed. Send an e-mail to spamreport@google.com or spamcrusader@inktomi.com.

4.   Pay-Per-Click

> Why use pay-per-click when you are already
> registered with search engines?

There is another way to get ranked highly in search engines. This can put you at the top of a search engine nearly instantly. Pay-Per-Click (PPC), also called Paid Placement, is a paid advertising service that places your ad on a search engine.

- In Search Engine Optimization (SEO), you tweak the HTML and hope that the search engine will index your webpages. You also hope the search engine will use your carefully crafted sales pitch. But you have very little control over the results. In PPC, you pay to play. You have complete control over the text to be displayed. Placement is based on how much you pay. The more you pay, the higher your ad will be placed.

PPC generally means using the Google AdWords and Overture ad placement services. With both of these services, you place a bid and your ad is displayed according to the other bids within the same category.

First, let's look at an AdWord. In the following illustration there are three ads at the right side of the Google results page under Sponsored Links. These have a heading, two lines of text, and a URL.

These are paid ads from three different koi companies. If you click one of these, you will go to that company's website. When you click, Google charges that company a fee for the click. If the company bids

25¢, then Google charges 25¢ for the click.

Google displays only eight ads per page. If you go to the second page, you'll see eight more ads.

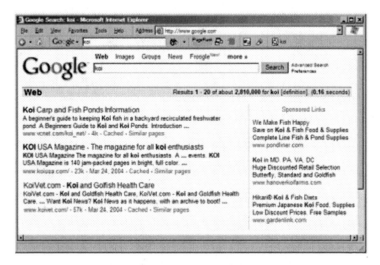

Here's what happens when you sign up for an AdWords account at Google:

- You create a small AdWords button. The AdWord has a title, two lines of text, and the URL.

- You add a list of keywords. When visitors at Google search for these, your ad is displayed. If a visitor clicks your ad, your website comes up.

- You set the daily maximum for your budget. If you set this at $2, then Google will display your ads until you reach $2 in clicks and then it stops for the day. Google spreads the ads across the day, so you won't use up your entire budget in the morning.

- Depending on what you bid for that particular keyword, Google will charge your account for the click. If you bid 12¢, Google charges you 12¢ for the click.

- The account is linked to your credit card. When Google bills you, they deduct it directly from your credit card.

- AdWords has elaborate reporting tools that show you the number of clicks, the percentage of views versus clicks, the cost per click, your ad's average position, and whether the visitor was converted to buying.

What are the drawbacks of Pay-Per-Click?

- PPC can be expensive. If the category is crowded, others will bid competitively for the top spots.

- PPC is a temporary solution. In a long-term strategy, PPC does not get a webpage into the core of the web. It does not add the webpage to a community. If you rely on PPC, you will forget how search engines work and your website will not be in the core of your category.

- Search Engine Optimization (SEO) companies prefer PPC because they can charge a commission for this service.

- Old-school marketing prefers PPC because this is the way they've been selling advertising for decades. Did television ads produce any results? Who cares? They got their commission.

- Companies prefer PPC because they are accustomed to paying for services. They assume that paid services (Business Class) are better than free services. By paying, they get control over ads, text, and placement.

All of these conspire to raise the costs of PPC. Companies will easily spend tens of thousands of dollars on PPC without checking the effectiveness of the PPC campaigns.

However, there are some very good reasons to use Pay-Per-Click:

- You pay, you play. You can get the top positions at the search engines.

- PPC is quick and easy. Depending on the size of your credit card, you can be at the top of the page at Google within 15 minutes.

- Most competitors don't use PPC, so you get placement above them. Although there are 2.9 million koi webpages, you can be listed at the top with a relatively small ad budget. With careful bid management, you can get great results for very little money.

- Google AdWords has very good tracking and reports. You can see what works and fix what doesn't work.

- PPC really works. AdWords bring traffic. You can track this in the AdWords statistics.

We've seen this over and over in nearly every field. There's very little competition. Only a fraction of companies are using AdWords. There are some 13 million registered companies in the USA. According to *Business Week* only about 200,000 advertisers were using AdWords at Google in April 2004.

When you start working with AdWords and look at your competitors in your market space, you'll notice most of those AdWord campaigns are not effective. Google is secretive about AdWords and their help pages are not very helpful. If you design a good e-commerce strategy, which includes AdWords, you should be able to improve traffic and revenues. With AdWords, every action can be tracked. There are detailed statistics for everything that happens with your ads.

- When you create the ads, don't create just one or two— create 12 to 15. Don't worry too much over what goes into the ad. Try all sorts of variations and ideas. Try flippant ads, silly ads, and flat ads. Run the ads for a week or so and look at the results. The ads will be sorted by click rates and you'll see exactly how each ad works. For whatever reason, people will click on ad #5 but will ignore ad #2. The market will tell you which one is best.

This is a problem for ad agencies. They bring in someone with 20 years of experience to write your ads. Or you get an intern to make twelve ads with different texts, random stuff, try this and that. Which one does a better job? Google AdWords will show you what the market actually prefers. Just create the ads, throw them out to the masses, and see what they go for.

It's always surprising which ad is the winner. You can't predict. It's also surprising that there can be a large difference in response rate to ads with nearly the same words.

- It's hard to sit down and create 12 different ads. We've found it works best if you don't think about it. Just create all sorts of variations. In one ad, put line A and B, in the next ad, reverse them. Mix up the words.

Someone could probably write a text randomizer that lets you type your keywords and adds a bunch of sales lines and mixes them up. Stuck for ideas on writing your AdWords? There's a useful little book with lists of marketing phrases. *Phrases that Sell*, by Werz and Germain, has over 5,000 phrases divided into some 80 categories. It also includes two chapters on how to write marketing copy.

- AdWords is Darwin's Survival of the Fittest in action. Create at least 12 ads and see which produces a higher click-through rate (CTR). Delete the weak ads. If an ad works, don't change it. Create variations of the successful ads and see which ones work. Run the campaign for at least 1,000 impressions. You need about that many ad views to draw a meaningful conclusion. Delete the weak ads and create more.

Google displays AdWords to users when the ad's keywords match the user's search terms. Google also displays ads to users when the ad's keywords are related to the user's search terms. For example, if the user searches for tennis shoes, Google will offer ads for tennis shoes. This is an example of Google's CIRCA technology, which is able to match terms that are relevant, related, or in the same category. This means when you are coming up with your list of keywords, you should think of related concepts, terms, synonyms, and so on. Try as many keywords as possible. Use your Adwords account to delete the words that don't produce traffic.

- Here are some problems to avoid:

- In the first week or two, Google's grammar patrol will complain about your ads. They are very picky. When they send you a notice that your ad doesn't meet their guidelines, just modify the ads.
- Do not add dozens of keywords at once. This will lead to a low average CTR and Google will turn off the ad.

- Don't forget logarithmic distribution of page views. The large majority of users see only the first page. Your AdWord should ideally be in the top three positions.

- Marketing departments are accustomed to $50,000 ad campaigns and they will power bid to get the #1 spot. The max is $20 per click, but there's no maximum on the daily cap. If you get into a bidding war for the #1 spot, it can get very expensive. Positions #2 or #3 are just as visible to the users and are cheaper.

The daily cap isn't a solid number. If you cap your budget at $20 per day, you might end up paying slightly more on some days. Google may adjust this up or down during the month, but all in all, you won't pay more than $20 per day for the number of days in that month. In January, this can be $620 (31 days) and in February it can be $560 (at 28 days). This isn't much of a difference, but it can become significant for clients with $500 daily budgets. Depending on the number of days in a month, their monthly costs can range from $14,000 to $15,500.

The visitor is searching for a product. She took the initiative to type the words into a search engine. She chose to click on your AdWord. When she comes to your webpage, you immediately show her what she is looking for. She doesn't want to read your website's front page. She wants to buy a koi now.

The landing page must be highly relevant to the user's search. If the landing page is not relevant, she will go to the next website. The AdWord should point to a landing page that is tailored to the ad. You must create a landing page with relevant information that will convert the customer. The URL may read Koi-Heaven.com, but when users click, it'll send them to koi-heaven.com/buy-koi.html where there is a photo, a description, and a Buy Now button.

- Create specific ads for each product. If you're selling Koromo koi (a breed of koi), then create an AdGroup just for Koromo koi, put koromo in your keyword list and advertisement, and then point the ad to a unique landing page, such as koi-heaven.com/buy-koromo-koi.html, where the visitor sees a photo of a Koromo, reads about Koromo, and can fill out his name and credit card information on the same page.

- The landing page has to allow a short and simple transaction. The longer the page and the more steps, the more buyers you will lose. Review the ads every day for the first 21 days and every week after that. Aim for a 1% (or higher) click-through rate. If you're not getting at least this level, adjust your campaigns.

This strategy moves the emphasis away from the website. For the last ten years, the focus was on websites as a set of pages with information about the products, pages about the company, help pages, contact pages, and so on. Graphics designers built websites as a consistent set of pages. This approach was based on the company's perception of itself or the graphic designer's concept of a unified message.

However, as we've seen, search engines don't index websites. They index webpages. For the purpose of ranking high in a search engine, the emphasis should be on creating an informative webpage and getting other webpages to link to it. The user who is looking to buy a product or service is not searching for a website. She is looking for that particular product or service because it fits her needs. The webpage should be customer-centric. What is the customer's need? How does the webpage fulfill that need?

If the landing page is customer-centric, most customers will arrive, find their need is fulfilled, and buy. A few customers want to look around, and for them the website should include the usual pages about the company, background, answers, and so on. The emphasis, however, should be on the customer.

You can set up an AdWords campaign ahead of time and have it ready to start on the product release date. Create the campaign, select the keywords, write the ads, and then put the campaign on Pause. To pause a campaign, select the AdGroup and click Pause. This turns off the campaign. On the morning of product launch, remove the pause on the campaign.

AdWords are nearly instantaneous. When you turn these on, people will see them within minutes. In comparison, it can take weeks or even months for a website to get highly ranked.

We built a website for a client who was about to release a new $65,000 enterprise software product. While we were building and testing the website, we prepared the Adwords campaign and put it on pause. When everything was tested and finally ready, we turned on the AdWords campaign. Within 45 minutes, he had his first request for a product demonstration.

Another great feature of AdWords is its reports. AdWords includes a powerful reporting tool. This lets you keep track of your campaigns. You can create reports to show the effectiveness of your ads, the results, and the conversion rates. You can also set up the feature to send a report to you every week or every day. You should use this at the start of every campaign.

5.   *AdWords Acronyms*

> AdWords provides a great service for getting noticed on the web?

Google adds yet more terms, abbreviations, and acronyms. Here's an explanation of some of them:

Clicks: Every time someone clicks on your AdWord, that's one click.

> **Impr:** Impression. When the Adword is displayed to someone, that's an impression. It doesn't mean she saw it, but she had the opportunity to see it—just as when you're browsing through a magazine and there is an advertisement for a Honda, that's an impression whether you noticed it or not.

> **CTR:** Click-through rate. This is the number of people who clicked on the ad, compared to the number of impressions. The CTR is stated as a percentage. If the AdWord was displayed 100 times and 25 people clicked it, that's a 25% CTR.

> **CPC:** cost per click. This is what you bid to pay for each click. However, the actual amount will be lower.

> **Avg CPC:** The average cost per click: based on a daily average of the CPCs. If this is significantly lower than your CPC bid, you should adjust your bids.

Cost: The total that you're paying for that AdWord. This is the number of clicks multiplied by the actual CPC.

Conv. Rate: If you set up Conversion Tracking (strongly recommended), this column reports the percentage of visitors who bought a product.

Cost/Conv: Cost per converison shows the total costs of your campaign against each click. If the overall cost was $12 for 50 clicks and you made two sales, both of those sales cost you $6 each in advertising. This is the most significant number on the page: your Cost/Conv should be within the range that you're willing to pay for advertising the product. If this number is greater than your profits, you're losing money on the sale.

That last item needs a bit more explanation. Let's say we're selling offspring from our award-winning koi. To raise Koi-san, it takes 25 pounds of koi food pellets, 2,000 gallons of bottled Japanese spring water, and so on. We add that up and it costs $50 for one year. We decide to sell the koi for $100. Our profit margin will be $50.

Therefore, we should be willing to spend a percentage of that profit on advertising the koi. How much? If we allocate $25 in advertising (in other words, another cost), we end up with a $25 profit. If we spend $60 per koi in advertising, we've lost money on the koi.

Remarkably, many people set their advertising budget on a guess. "Oh, $500 per month sounds about right." With AdWords, you can see the effectiveness of a campaign, which lets you justify the advertising budget. If the advertising is effective—that is, if it produces revenues and profit—you can increase the budget.

To set an initial advertising budget, calculate the advertising cost per item that you're willing to spend (how much you're willing to spend to make one sale), the number of sales you expect to make each month, and then work backward to set the monthly budget, the daily budget, and the bid price. After a month of results, you can look at the conversion tracking and adjust the budget.

AdWords can do more than just sell products. You can use AdWords to create mailing lists. Write the AdWords with text such as Free Newsletter and point this to your newsletter signup page. If you are preparing a product and the release date is months away, you can start early by building a mailing list of potential customers.

6.   *Writing the Ads*

Ads should be based on your keywords in order to get noticed more often.

Use your list of keywords. Use the keywords for the title and body text. Use capitalization in the URL. Instead of writing koi-heaven.com, use Koi-Heaven.com. This is easier to read.

- Look at the AdWords of your top competitors. Print out their ads and use their text to get ideas to create new ads. If appropriate, include your price in the ad. This deters unqualified buyers. If you write that koi are $500 each, buyers who are looking for $1 koi will go elsewhere. You save money if they don't click on your ad.

- Use phrases that invoke positive emotions. Examples: Free, cheap, sale, tricks, you, tips, fact, learn, discover, free shipping, fast, easy, convenient, best, sexy, quick, fun, instantly, save time, powerful, save money, most popular.

- Use phrases with a call-to-action. Examples: Buy today, save 50%, download free trial now, sale ends tomorrow, sale-priced, special offer, limited offer, and similar.

- Negative ads which evoke fear or worry are not as effective as positive ads. Negative words and phrases include: avoid, worried about . . . , bankruptcy, don't get caught . . . , and so on. Don't mislead. Users strongly dislike deceptive or misleading links that get them to click on a link. They will instantly back out and return to the search engine. For more, see the Consumers Union study mentioned in the Introduction.

There are several ways to enter the keywords. You can add quotation marks around the words, use square brackets, or nothing at all. Here's an explanation from Google for each one:

Broad match: Enter your keywords, such as tennis shoes. Your ad will show when users search on tennis and shoes, in any order, even if the query includes other terms, such as tennis rackets and running shoes. Google also uses expanded matching. This means Google will use other relevant terms and variations (such as tennis sneakers).

Phrase match: Place quotes around your keyword "tennis shoes." Your ad shows when users search for tennis shoes in that order and with other search terms. For example, your ad will show for red tennis shoes but not for the phrase shoes for tennis.

Exact match: Place brackets around your keyword: [tennis shoes]. Your ad will show when users search for tennis shoes in this order without other terms. For example, your ad won't show for the queries red tennis shoes or tennis bags and shoes.

Negative keyword: Include a dash before your keywords, such as -red. If your keyword phrase is tennis shoes and your negative keyword is -red, your ad will not show if a user searches for red tennis shoes.

Google will suggest a bid and a daily budget, but these are just guesses from Google. They have no idea of your sales volume or advertising margins. Estimate how many units you will sell in one month and then use your advertising margin to calculate the monthly advertising budget. Use this to set the daily budget. Set the bid to 5¢ and then adjust upwards to get into the top three positions.

For example, we expect to sell 50 koi at $100 each per month. We're willing to pay $10 to advertise each koi, so that's a monthly advertising budget of $500 ($10 per koi for 50 koi). Divide $500 by 30 days and that's $16.66 dollars per day. So we set the daily budget at $16.66. Now we adjust the bids to get our AdWords at the top of the list.

The major task in AdWords is to adjust your bids to keep your costs down and your ad position up. Your ad should be in the first five ads on the first page for your category. Due to logarithmic numbers, traffic falls very fast after the first page.
The bid price is not a simple number. The actual amount you'll pay depends on the bids from other advertisers.

Let's say there are only three companies with AdWords in the koi market. Apple bids $15, Berry bids $10, and Cherry bids 5¢. The actual price each company will pay is 1¢ plus the next lowest bid. The best way to explain this is with an example. Laura clicks on all three ads. What does each company pay for that click? Start at the bottom of the table and work up.

Company	They Bid	They Really Pay	Why They Pay That Amount
Apple	$15.00	$10.01	Apple pays the next lowest bid (Berry's $10 bid) plus 1¢. Apple pays $10.01.
Berry	$10.00	$00.06	Berry pays the next lowest bid (Cherry's 5¢ bid) plus 1¢, so Berry pays 6¢.
Cherry	$00.05	$00.05	Cherry bid 5¢, so he pays 5¢.

If you look carefully, you'll see Ms. Berry and Mr. Cherry are paying pennies for their ads, but Mr. Apple is paying $10.01 for his ad. You can wildly overpay if you don't manage your bids.

If you misunderstand this bidding system, your campaign can be severely affected. If both Apple and Berry have a $20 daily budget, Apple will get only two AdWords displays ($20 divided by $10 = 2), but Berry will get 330 displays ($20 divided by 6¢ = 330). Although Ms. Berry and Mr. Cherry are bidding less than Mr. Apple, they will sell more koi.

7. *AdGroups*

> If you create dozens of campaigns you should consider AdGroups.

One of the challenges of Google AdWords is the multiple levels of Campaigns, AdGroups, and AdWords. It takes some time to become familiar with this feature. Some people create dozens of campaigns, with a single AdWord in each campaign. Others put all the Adwords within the same AdGroup. When you enter into your Google AdWord account, you click on a campaign. This brings you down to the AdGroup level. You click on an AdGroup and this brings you down to the AdWord level.

- **Campaign:** Used to create various campaigns and set the overall daily maximum for each campaign. For example, you can set the maximum at $10 per day for a campaign. If you're selling different products, then create a campaign for each product. The Koi-Campaign for koi and the Turtle-Campaign for turtles.

- **AdGroup:** Within the campaign, you create AdGroups. Each AdGroup can be for a sub-product. For the koi, there would be the Red-Koi-AdGroup, the White-Koi-AdGroup, and so on.

- **AdWord:** Within each AdGroup, you create several AdWords. This is a group of keywords that will trigger any of the Adwords ads. You should create at least nine ads for the set. The keywords will include koi, ornamental fish, and so on.

Use the Campaigns to control the overall spending for a product line. Create different AdGroups. Each AdGroup contains the products within that group. Within the AdGroup, create the AdWords.

For example, you sell koi and you also offer repair services: roof repair and plumbing. Create two campaigns: one for koi and the second for repairs. Within the first, create four AdGroups for the four kinds of koi that you raise. Within the second, create two AdGroups, one for each service. This lets you control the costs for each campaign.

8.   *Content Targeting at AdSense*

Making money with AdSense.

Google has an affiliate program called AdSense. People sign up and Google displays Adwords on their webpages, where the webpage is related to the search terms. When visitors click on an ad, Google gives part of the click fee to the sponsor website.

For example, someone is looking at a koi website. On the side of the page, the Google AdWords are listed, including your AdWord. The visitor clicks on the AdWord to learn more about your koi. You pay a click fee to Google, and Google gives part of that to the website. The problem with Content Targeting is that visitors didn't necessarily arrive at that page by searching, so they are not highly motivated. You will pay for those clicks anyway. You should experiment with Content Targeting. If it works for your website, then it's okay. If not, you can turn it off.

Gmail, Google's free e-mail, similar to Hotmail and Yahoo! free e-mail accounts, is another way for Google to increase the display of AdWords. Google will look for keywords in e-mails and then insert related advertising into the e-mail. For example, you write to your friends about plans to go bass fishing. Gmail will insert Google AdWords advertising that is related to bass fishing. Gmail includes Google search, so when people search their e-mails, another Google AdWord will be displayed.

One of the best features in AdWords is the conversion tracking. A click on your ad is nice, but what really counts is when the visitor buys your product. This is a conversion from visitor to buyer. From the dotcom crash, we learned that traffic is irrelevant. Who cares if you have 16 million visitors? The only thing that counts on an e-commerce site is sales.

AdWords offers a free conversion tracking tool. You fetch a bit of HTML code at AdWords and place it in your website's thank-you page. This is the page that a customer sees when he has finished making a purchase. This lets AdWords know that the visitor clicked on the AdWord, came to your site, and bought the product. The conversion tracking shows the number of conversions, the percentage, and the total cost per conversion.

You can also track the lead generation. If you use the website to capture names for your mailing list, the conversion tracking will show the number of leads, the effectiveness of the lead conversion, and the total costs of the lead generation campaign.

9.   *The Media Buy*

How different is an online media buy from the regular media buying for print?

You may find a conflict of interest out there surrounding "the media buy." PPC creates a conflict of interest between the client and the SEO company. In traditional marketing, the ad agency sets its fee on a percentage of the media buy. If the client buys $100,000 worth of advertising in TV media, then the ad agency charges, for example, 30% as its commission, which would be $30,000.

This means that the more the client spends, the more the agency gets. There is little incentive for the agency to convince the client to buy less. In fact, it would be against the agency's interests. Any employee who tells a client to spend less money will soon be looking for a new job.

- The tracking and reporting tools in PPC offer a solution. Instead of basing the fee on a percentage of money spent, agencies should charge a percentage of the revenues generated by the ad campaign. This gives the agency an incentive to improve the campaign: the better the results, the more they earn.

The first bid PPC service was Overture. Overture is a different animal with a unique approach to bidding when using their services. It is widely used among SEO companies. However, we don't use it, for several reasons:

- Overture does not use search relevancy. Your ads are displayed regardless of relevancy. This will lead to more clicks but less conversion.

- Overture doesn't penalize underperforming ads, unlike Google. If your ads aren't performing well in Google AdWords, they will shut off your account. In a way, that's annoying, but Google also obligates you to improve your campaign. Both you and Google earn more.

Overture places your links into search engines such as AltaVista, Go.com, Infospace.com, IWon.com, MSN, and Yahoo! The first four search engines have low market share. At MSN, it's difficult to tell the difference between paid links and search engine results. Considering the reactions from users in the Consumers Union report and studies that show that users only look at the first ten links, it's not too promising.

But who knows? Go ahead and try it. You might get better results.

So what is the best SEO strategy—technical or content? Modify the HTML code or add ten articles to your website? In the beginning of this chapter, we wrote that 85% of searches are for information. In order to have the highest number of users, the search engines compete with each other to offer the best results, which means the best information for each search.

- Google wants to see useful information. This means information that is so good that other sites link to it. So add information to your site, get other sites to link to you, and Google will rank you higher.

- If you do only technical SEO by modifying the HTML code, your site will be at risk of falling in the rankings. Search engines don't like it when people use tricks to modify their ranking. If a method is being abused too much, the search engines will block that method. The websites that were based on that trick will fall off the charts.

Google changed their search engine in late 2003 and early 2004 to improve the ranking of informational webpages. Webpages by universities, colleges, magazines, and dissertations went up in ranking, sites with something for sale slid down.

10.   *Adding Content*

How many pages is the right number of pages
for a website?

Also be aware of the amount of content you are adding. Many corporate sites are actually very small. They have perhaps 15 to 20 pages. There just simply isn't very much there to be indexed. You should plan to add at least 25 to 50 pages of content. Ideally, you should have several hundred pages. This is not unrealistic.

- These articles can be about your company, your products, your services, your industry, the history of your industry, overviews of the industry, stories about customers and clients, trends, projections, reviews, analysis, and so on. The articles should be customer-centric, presenting information that your customers want to see, not just marketing text. Don't just offer your product. Explain how to cure fungus on koi. Describe the home remedies. If the information is useful, other sites will link to it. The articles don't need to be long—they can be one or two pages each.

When you write these articles, don't forget to use your SEO skills. Weave your list of keywords, your sales pitch, and other information into the texts. The articles should be rich in keywords so the search engines can easily identify the appropriate cluster and then index your pages. Give your keyword list to your writers and ask them to use these words in the article.

To get articles for your website, you can hire professional writers and journalists. You can name the writer as the article's author, but often, with the writer's consent, you can put the CEO's name on it. Just as the speeches of CEOs are usually written by professional writers, so are the articles signed by CEOs and CTOs at many websites.

- Contact industry magazines and trade journals and ask their editors if they can suggest a writer for your project. Often one of the staff writers will write the articles for you, under his name or an assumed name.

- Hire writers from the National Writers Union (NWU). Its membership includes 3,500 professional business writers and technical writers who write articles for hundreds of business magazines. See nwu-resumebank.com and nwu.org/hotline.
- Ask your fans—people who are passionate about your products or industry—to write articles.

214 – Blueprints for Success - eMarketing

Checklists

List the links on your home page that point to information pages on your site.

_____

_____

_____

_____

_____

How often do you update your home page?

_____

_____

Check your Google index date for your home page. What date is displayed?

_____

_____

List your most popular pages on your site.

_____

_____

_____

_____

_____

Write 5 ads you could use for Google AdWords.

_____

_____

_____

_____

_____

_____

_____

_____

_____

List 10 keywords you would use for your website.

_____

_____

_____

_____

_____

NOTES

10. The Family of Deliverables

1. What You Can Offer Your Clients

Key strategies.

In this final chapter we'll take a look at what you can offer your clients. We'll touch on some key strategies that can generate return on investment and also encourage clients to invest in you and your company.

We'll take a look at some strategies that have already been mentioned in this book and go into them in more detail and we'll also introduce you to some new, easy to use techniques and steps that will help you not only land the client but keep the client.

For more information on any of the following solutions or deliverables, go to www.hartcreativemarketing.com. If your questions remain unanswered, feel free to call us at Hart Creative Marketing, Inc. 925.705.0372.

2. Email Letterhead

Key strategies.

Hart Creative Marketing, Inc. does not send their professional correspondence on plain white paper, and they decided their e-mails shouldn't be any different. It's **letterhead for your everyday e-mail**.

Top reasons are listed below why companies of any size are not abandoning the brand consistency while sending one-to-one e-mails. Each day we average 25 one-to-one e-mails. They present one opportunity to illuminate your receiver of any and all values you offer. There may be no greater opportunity to hold receivers of your e-mail captive for a moment, enticing them to click through and sign up, download a deliverable, and even buy from you directly from the e-mail letterhead.

1. **Branding.** Maintain consistency with brand strategy and visual identity.

2. **Differentiate.** Modernize your communications. Capitalize on the multitude of messages your company sends daily and lead with your best impression every time.

3. **Interactivity.** Recipients can click on template links to reach online destinations including digital collateral.

4 **Results.** Drive qualified visitors to relevant pages on your website to recoup existing investment (ROI).

5 **Measurability.** Tracking measures the impact branded e-mail has on your audience. Web-based reporting of key metrics, such as clicks and v-card downloads, is included.

6 **Compactness.** Adds less than a kilobyte to e-mails, which insures rapid delivery with minimal bandwidth.

7 **Ease of use.** Ready to deploy in weeks. Minimal effort required for enterprise-wide usage. Utilizes existing infrastructure for trouble-free implementation.

8 **Quality assurance.** You're in complete control of your brand. A centralized, web-based administrative system hosts the technology in a manner that your staff can easily manage.

9 **Economical.** Like paper letterhead, cost is measured in fractions of a cent per message. Price models are generally per employee. Volume discounts can apply based on the number of end user licenses.

Come to www.hartcreativemarketing.com to find out more on the eMarketing deliverable that will give you the best return on your dollar compared with almost any e-mail technology on the market.

3.   *Video Email*

> Web presentation enables you to present a more compelling proposition.

Television commercials have long been the staple of large-budget advertising campaigns. Now your clients can leverage the powerful results of video commercials at a fraction of the cost. Your largest untapped audience is the one that comes to your site on a daily basis. Traffic from web commercials can be turned into actionable leads by promoting subscriptions or requests for contact from a sales or service representative.

Envision a television-like spot that tells your story accurately and concisely—one that shares the vision of the business and includes clips of real customers describing how the company has positively impacted their lives. The commercial could also include any mentions of your business in the press. There could be a few different versions with private-labeling and custom endings for use through any distribution channels. Your distribution channel partners could play the commercial in-store and online to influence buyers and trigger a purchase.

Can you deliver flawless training and sales presentations every time on demand? The video presentation enables you to present a more compelling proposition to all channel partners and affiliates. The commercial will ensure that the viewer will experience the best sales presentation every time privately and conveniently via the internet. A web presentation enables the audience to "sell" themselves and be persuaded by their own inferences and conclusions. It simulates a "face-to-face" presentation without the time, expense, and inconvenience of meetings or conferences.

Web presentation enables you to present a more compelling proposition to more channel partners. The power of multimedia can have a dramatic impact on message comprehension and retention. Educating and informing these prospects with a concise commercial will enable your clients to harvest a higher percentage of qualified channel partners and enable the conversion of more sales through informed, educated, and motivated distributors.

4.   *Sales, PR, Branded Web Templates*

> How do you most cost-effectively distribute valuable
> sales collateral and business communications?

Digital media packets delivered in amplified multimedia messages using Flash, video, and HTML can reduce reliance on costly and ineffective traditional methods like print collateral, direct mail, and impersonal mass e-mail campaigns.

We can help you achieve better return on investment, response rates, and conversion rates. You'll be pleased with faster production and immediate delivery. And you'll love the less-costly production rates, distribution, and management. A sales and PR web-based template is most commonly an extension of your existing website that has content that speaks directly to the visitor's needs: easy to load, easy to read, easy to interact with you, and, most of all, the user can find what he or she needs fast.

Make no mistake, eliminating collateral you hold in your hand would be nonproductive. Integrated marketing demands a variety of collateral that best serves the audience you're reaching. They control the purchase you want them to make and have specific media styles and formats that meet their preferences. A brochure may have as much impact on a sales call as does the e-mail you deliver following your meeting to educate the prospect even further.

You will increase responsiveness and effectiveness with cost-effective messaging applications. This state-of-the-art technology will provide your employees, business partners, and resellers a means to personalize and deploy branded, informative digital media packets through a web-based interface.

Digital media packets are managed centrally within your organization to provide consistent, effective communication tools for on-demand distribution of sales materials. HTML formatted e-mail messages contain "virtual attachments" that provide unlimited flexibility for distribution of sales collateral. Because they are downloaded directly from a server instead of sent as attachments in each e-mail, they save valuable inbox space. Message sizes with video and unlimited virtual attachments can be as low as 5K.

Real-time tracking increases sales force business intelligence, digital distribution of collateral lowers costs, rich media is impressive and effective, and viral components encourage distribution throughout your prospect's company.

5. *HartSmart E-Sender, Expert Marketing*

> **Build lifetime relationships and get people to take action.**

The mandate for today's marketers is clear: build lifetime relationships, but get people to take action . . . now! E-mail marketing is fast, inexpensive, targeted, effective, and trackable. In fact, the e-mail channel has emerged as one of the most profitable and economical ways for your clients to manage their customer relationships. It's important that your clients continue to regularly communicate with subscribers and deliver e-mail messages that are of value to the recipients.

Below are some of the deliverables that Hart Creative Marketing, Inc., offers their clients:

Auto responders will deliver an automatic response via e-mail to any touch point on your website. User interacts with you and receives a follow-up message—the ultimate opportunity to further up-sell, educate, request one to forward your message, etc.

Monthly e-newsletters will continue to keep consumers apprised of your client's complete product portfolio and help to automate cross-selling and up-selling efforts. Think of this deliverable as a way to offer consistent branding via a trackable, personalized mini-website. Enhancement will include an updated design, more customer testimonials, news and events, industry affiliations, etc. Newsletters might have customized content based on the opt-in category selection for each individual. Your clients can also launch a channel partner newsletter (sent quarterly or seasonally) to allow potential and existing domestic and international distributors to remain informed of company announcements, product introductions, promotional ideas, marketing recommendations, channel success stories, testimonials, press releases, etc.

Event-based e-mails will connect your clients with potential and existing customers year round; for example, e-mailing gift suggestions around the many national holidays (Valentine's Day, Mother's Day, etc.). Additionally, a birthday e-mail and customer anniversary e-mail are also planned. Each of these communications allows your clients to contact their customers in a relevant and meaningful way. The extra touches at times make the sale or contribute to relationship building and brand loyalty.

Special offers can be e-mailed to your client's key audiences. Additionally, customer appreciation e-mails might be sent to high-value consumers who have made large purchases. Finally, a thank-you e-mail may be sent to registered consumers every time they visit the website, asking if their needs have been fully met.

Press releases sent via e-mail enable your clients to blast featured announcements and stories to a wide range of constituents. Oftentimes, people miss an article published in a daily journal or on a website. E-mailing the story the same day or after an article is published allows your client's audience to view the information they might have missed reading elsewhere or serves to remind those who have already been privy to the daily press.

Direct e-mails can significantly reduce labor, time, and associated costs. E-mails can be used at key times to connect with busy potential and existing customers. E-mailing will strengthen brand awareness and provide a convenient alternative channel for dialog between your clients and their customers. E-mails could be used to highlight services and link back to desired areas on your client's website.

Test e-mails present an opportunity for your clients to test various segments' receptiveness to opting-in, calls to action, creative work, and special offers to A-list customers. Your clients can be presented with results before launching costly online and/or offline campaigns.

Transaction e-mails are crucial for relationship building. An example is sending an automated, personalized HTML e-mail immediately following a registration for your client's electronic newsletter. The message can be very simple: "Congratulations! You have signed up for the [Client's Name] e-newsletter." Sometimes the extra little touches can make all the difference to a new or potential customer.

Alerts and auto reminders can be distributed to gain the attention of constituents regarding time-sensitive considerations. For example, consider sending an e-mail notifying members of new offerings of interest and value to them. Create a sense of urgency and trigger action via time-sensitive e-mails (e.g., "Reply before X date to secure your free Y valued at Z").

6. Email Delivery Systems

Key strategies.

Hart Creative Marketing, Inc., supplies all the e-mail technology our clients need to design, develop, test, launch, manage, and track successful e-mail marketing campaigns. We have a package that can fit your budget. Visit us at www.hartcreativemarketing.com to start sending your e-mails with the
HartSmart E-Sender.

We continue to supply our clients with the expertise and all the tools needed to create and launch superior e-mail marketing campaigns, including advanced personalization, dynamic content, multi-part MIME delivery (AOL, text, HTML), bounce management, unsubscribe services, data warehousing, central campaign management, privacy policies, local, state, and federal compliances, preview and extensive testing before sending, 24/7 access to real-time tracking, and comprehensive reporting.

In fact, our technologies deliver, track, and report every click and HTML e-mail message viewed by every recipient. Specifically, they collect timestamps, browser versions, clicked URLs, image SRCs, bounces, and detailed bounce causes, opt-ins, opt-outs, number of e-mails successfully sent, history of e-mails received by recipient, forward tracking, and change of address. We also track forward-to-friend messages separately from the original recipients. All of this information is available in real-time at any time from a secured online "read-only" reporting view. We can even e-mail reports to clients on a set schedule, if desired.

Through precise tracking and analysis, we'll know how many people are opening our clients' e-mails, what they are reading, what client software they are using (HTML, text-based, AOL), and where they go after they leave the e-mail. We use a unique combination of actual consumer click stream data and powerful analytic capabilities to develop insight into consumer online behavior. Our holistic approach enables us to improve database segmentation, messaging, and personalization.

7.   Selling Landing Pages

Promotions are only good when someone responds.

E-mail promotions are only as effective as the pages they drive users to. The online buying experience will be dramatically enhanced by leveraging a powerful "one-two" combo, the promotional e-mail and landing page. Historically, performance results have shown that simple promotional e-mails with a single call-to-action are among the most effective communications. Industry data show that using these communications to drive users to landing pages can dramatically improve return on investment.

Hart Creative Marketing, Inc., produces expertly designed landing pages that support promotional e-mail themes and timely product placements. For example, pairing two similar items could provide the basis of a powerful promotion. Holiday, seasonal, and special offers and new collections are all examples that would justify the custom development of unique selling pages.

8.   Teleseminars/Webinars

Online business starters.

Teleseminars are a great way to start your online business development marketing.

Why? They're more affordable than presenting your offerings or education by means of a Webinar. Teleseminars are less intimidating, as you are not speaking to the Power Point you're referring too while speaking online. Technology costs for teleseminars have dropped precipitously over the years. So no excuses, have courage and get out there and share your message with the world.

Webinars are an excellent way to educate prospects and move them further along in your sales process. They are cost-effective, provide a global reach, and are an excellent "offer" for lead generation campaigns. No wonder these events are growing at an unprecedented rate of over 20% per year. According to *PC Magazine*, executives believe that a vendor who invites them to a web conference is technologically savvy, respectful of their time and budget, and smart and efficient. But delivering a successful webinar can be a challenge. How can you improve attendance? What if you run into technical difficulties? Here are some practical "before, during, and after" tips to make your next webinar a success.

Before: Planning Your Webinar

- **Select your vendor**
  Not all webinar hosting vendors are alike. Choose a vendor that works with a variety of operating systems and is reliable and scalable. Also, consider vendors experienced in the latest techniques in application sharing, polling, chat, and recording features.

  Some vendors also provide targeted opt-in e-mail lists that are bundled with the webinar hosting.

- **Engage the help of a meeting consultant**
  Vendors such as Intercall, which offers Webex, Placeware, and other offerings, provide meeting consultants as part of their service. These consultants will educate you on best practices, train you on how to conduct a successful webinar, and be present during the webinar to assist with any issues that may arise.

  Choose a meeting moderator to assist the speaker or speakers. Intercall offers moderators trained by CNN for a truly professional performance.

- **Select dates and times to maximize attendance**
  Plan to host the webinar at least twice to accommodate different time zones. Avoid Mondays or Fridays as these are peak conferencing days and attendance is also often lower.

  Start at 10 to 15 minutes past the hour. Most meetings end on the hour and this offset gives your participants time to decompress before joining your meeting.

- **Prepare an exciting presentation**
  Invite an industry expert, customer, or partner to participate. This will stimulate more interest, drive participation, and create synergy.

  Don't cram too much type or information on your slides. Keep them simple and leave plenty of white space or background. You may also want to use sponsorships to defray your promotional costs or to expand your reach.

During: Conducting the Webinar

- **Practice webinar etiquette**
  Join your meeting early and verify that all links and presentations are working. Share a "welcome" slide that says your meeting will be starting shortly.

Before your meeting begins, provide a quick review of housekeeping items, such as how to use the chat feature, or how the Q&A session will be handled.

Have each speaker identify herself when speaking, and add a photo and bio of the speakers.

- **Avoid "Death by Powerpoint"**
  The most captivating presentations tend to be multimedia. Include animation, flash, photos, web-demos, or other visual aids to make your presentation more interesting.

  Engage your audience by including polling questions at key points in your presentation. This will help keep your audience's attention.

- **Survey attendees before and after the webinar**
  Ask qualifying questions during registration. This gives you keen insight into your audience. Use this information to tailor your presentation accordingly.

    - As people exit the webinar, ask them a short series of follow-up questions to further qualify them. Questions like these can provide timely information for your sales reps:
    - What did you like most about this presentation?
    - How likely are you to use this service?
    - Would you like a sales rep to contact you?

After: Leveraging Your Investment

- **Record the webinar and Q&A session**
  Post the webinar on your website for future viewing. Build a reference library of past webinars for your customers and prospects to peruse at their leisure.

  Recorded webinars and their Q&As can also be very helpful in training new employees or reviewing customer input prior to a new product launch, selling event, or internal business strategy session.

- **Follow up with every attendee and registrant**
  Send a follow-up e-mail to participants thanking them for their attendance. Include additional relevant information; invite them to the next webinar.

  Send a "sorry we missed you" e-mail to registrants who did not attend. Nurture these prospects to entice them to attend your next event.

- **Conduct a post-mortem**
  Review all feedback gathered from the webinar. Consider variations in the registration process, presentation, and Q&A process to determine what could make the webinar even more engaging.

Come to www.hartcreativemarketing.com to learn more and even sign up to do your own teleseminar/webinar.

Checklists

Which of the following do you have on your website?

Images
Flash
Audio
Plain Text
Links
Navigation Bar

What marketing collateral does your company currently produce (hard copy)?

_____

_____

_____

_____

_____

Which of these items could be better delivered on the web?

_____

_____

_____

_____

_____

What topics could you deliver as a Webinar?

_____

_____

_____

_____

_____

Who does the marketing for your company?

_____

_____

List all of the things for which you are willing to make a commitment regarding your website.

_____

_____

_____

_____

_____

_____

_____

_____

_____

_____

_____

_____

NOTES

Last Word

"What lies behind us and what lies before us are tiny matters compared to what lies within us"
—Ralph Waldo Emerson

In our life's journey, we constantly pursue goals and seek to achieve for ourselves what we want. Your blueprint to emarketing is a roadmap to reach those marketing objectives, and is intended to inspire you to face any marketing challenge with an attitude of gratitude. When gratitude is absent from your way of thinking day to day, you can end up feeling negative, edgy, fearful, or just plain nervous just thinking about marketing.

What I Discovered

I want to leave you with insight into how I overcome thoughts and behavior patterns that pull me away from attaining my goals, including writing this book, *Blueprint to eMarketing*. Those behavior patterns include lack of commitment, determination, and desire and inability to make decisions. I increased my success by focusing on what I was in control of and not placing attention on what I was not in control of. Not worrying about the outcome got me much more of what I've wanted in life. I discovered when I applied the same approach to other areas of my business marketing plans, again I would get more of what I wanted.

Look at the various areas of your business and imagine for a moment feeling confident and committed to your new marketing strategies and goals —excited to wake up each day and give your marketing garden another splash of your water, your energy, your passions. This transition is an incremental change within you that produces organic growth where one day you look around you and see all the fruits of your labor. Those fruits you see are from an attitude of gratitude that shifts your intent and language from "I wish" to "I will." To face my darkest days where I was the least interested in working on my enewsletter, or this book, or simply thinking about my marketing plans, I would say to myself, "I will set marketing goals that are realistic and complete them according to the agreement I set with myself." No more, no less. This removed all my fears and empowered me to believe I am successful and can accomplish any goal I set for myself. Notice I didn't say "I will *be* successful," rather " I *am* successful."

You may feel the same self pressure cooker I was sitting in when I knew I had marketing chores to do. For example, write content for an enewsletter, update content on my website, outline a white paper. Some days, it can take everything out of you to sit down and mentally step into your agreement by completing the tasks you agreed to complete. Completion does not mean the entire enewsletter has been written—maybe you started and hit writer's block. Do you think this is a setback, or even an abject failure? If you believe you failed because you hit a roadblock and could not complete the task you agreed to complete, then celebrate the failure. Too often we forget to embrace the failure, the point in which we were challenged. Embracing and celebrating the failure to complete any task will help keep you from giving up altogether. Giving up after a defeat, or even repeated defeats, is what makes that failure permanent. Failure is just a setback that reminds us that we must choose another path to achieve what we seek. That path is most often not far from the path you're on at the time you experience this fearful feeling called "failure."

Integrity Is a Skill
Integrity breeds consistency resulting in a self-marketing transition. A transition is an incremental change, an organic growth. At its core is your true self. This is your spirit and your burning desires to attain what you set out to do with a single mindedness of purpose where all your pretenses will melt away. The pretenses, if not addressed, will slow you down, give you the feeling of being disconnected from yourself, unable to gain any momentum to complete your marketing goals. For example, you'll start with an agenda to send out an enewsletter every month and within a short time you've stopped. Why? Because we all sabotage our own dreams of achievement by not honoring the very agreements we make with ourselves. I would ask that you look at integrity as something other than simply a value, albeit a very important one. I would have you consider viewing integrity also as a skill. To become an expert in dancing the Salsa, you must practice it daily. To become an expert practitioner of integrity, you must be practice it too every day.

Look around at the areas in your life you consider important to you—your relationships, fitness, personal wealth, and so on. I can tell you, my achievements in these areas were a very mixed bag at one time recently. I was in an often-repeated pattern that I would commit to goals, purse them vigorously and enthusiastically, and then inevitably tire of them and quit. Maybe what I had set out to do was the equivalent of a marathon, and I might even have gotten halfway through, but the lack of accomplishment (and therefore confidence) would remain.

Please take my gift to you: my lesson of understanding that integrity is a skill you apply to your marketing goals every day—the goals in the agreement you made with yourself; goals that were reached on a road full of failures; failures you embraced and celebrated that enabled you find a new path and not give up. Be consistent and never give up. Get that enewsletter out every month because it has great value to your customer base, and feel better about yourself in the process.

Integrity is a skill that applies directly to your ability to plow through the obstacles that make you feel disconnected from winning the internet marketing game. When I was disconnected from winning the internet marketing game and could turn my attitude around to get the task at hand completed, it was a good day. You can have the same sense of completion and confidence. Here's what you do.

When you are not following through on goals you set with yourself in an agreement, understand that your limitations are a result of your under-practiced and stagnant commitment to personal integrity. When you're suffering from the "midway" point, stopping halfway through a task to never return, the pain you feel is coming from knowing you only made it halfway through the task you set out to finish. This means your "skill" level in integrity is fairly mid-range and it's reflected in the accomplishments you achieved halfway. To increase your odds for success, reducing the number of times you hit this "midway" point will help you greatly in climbing the mountain of dreams you plan to hike.

What I hope you get from my "last word" is not what you found most often in this book, tips and tricks to building your business through the net, but rather inspiration and guidance to crash through your fears and understand the slow and patient process to successful marketing using the web. To crash through fears means tightening up your skill of integrity—enough to see and feel within you every day a change for the better: to stop the endless cycle of creating goals only to quit following the rule of integrity. For instance, place something in an agreement to help yourself with your marketing, and only set a goal you know you can complete. This is very important. And make this commitment only for one week at a time. Most people never begin to act on a dream they wish they could accomplish, because last time they tried they stopped halfway, leaving all their aspirations in frustration and disappointment.

Make it clear from now on that you must make your goals and objectives short and simple in order to begin. Make goals that are really easy so you can feel how invigorating it is to face fear and the unknowns of marketing when you complete your goals each week— one week of goals you know you can reach. Increase your skill set first and foremost in the practice of integrity and you too will stop the endless cycle of creating goals only to quit again.

There are many elements that go into building success, but without integrity your dreams and wishes remain just that. Resolve from this day forward that your integrity will be nothing short of a ten, and your goals and plans will take on true meaning.

NOTES

Resource Guide

The following lists are of resources you can use to increase your eMarketing activity. The books listed will allow you to delve deeper into some of the areas discussed in this book.

Online Marketing

People respond to email promotions not email announcements
Prepublication Sale – Allow us 3 weeks to deliver your book
Customer Appreciation Sales
Ebook Clearance Sale
50% off. This time your ½ off is $39.95 from $97.00.
Birthday sale. Turning 25. 25% off everything
Subscriber Only Sale
Create a club and deliver promotion offers and sell discounted products

Hover Ads - Upsell
Email me for the latest program hart@jerryhart.com
Doubled Subscription Rates the same day. Even add audio to Entry Pop Up.
Exit Pop Up Model. Only comes up if they exit. If they buy, the exit model turns off.
Hover promoting Financing. Took 70 viewings for 1 conversion

Thank you Page Upsell
Get your affiliate links on your Thank you page. Thank you for submitting your order, click here to continue shopping. Check out the amazing offers below.

Harris Trick - Upsell
Input from a survey form http://www.databack.com/   Offer FREE Report or Author Sneak Peak for interactive survey. Wait 24 hours before you send auto responder so it sounds honest. Also good for offline buyers who did not buy from you.
www.zoomerang.com   www.surveymonkey.com

Enews/5 Day Mini Course Sign Up Upsell
Thanks for signing up for HCM enews. In a few minutes you'll get the bonuses I promised you. Meantime, read this FREE report that leads to your product showcase.

EBook Creation

Creation and Copywriting http://www.elance.com
http://www.sunoasis.com (paid)
http://www.marketingtool.com

Discussion Boards

http://www.multicity.com
http://www.vbulletin.com
http://www.wowbb.com

Classified Ads

You can run classified ads. AOL can be very good because America Online has over 30 million subscribers. So if you have a product, you might try very inexpensive electronic classified ads to drive people to your website.

Streaming News

Another great way to get visitors to return is to have news. There are places out there that will send news directly to your site so people can simply check your website for their news. There are many different industry news feeds.

Some sites include:
http://www.7am.com
http://www.anaconda.net
http://www.wunderground.com/about/faq/weathersticker.asp

What's New

You can have a "what's new" portion of your website. Even better, "What's new in your industry?" You can have forms on your website so people can register for items or any events or "special sales" you might be holding. That gets them to come back. You might also include an ad for a new product or service on the registration form.

Once you get them there for any reason, you want to hit them again with something else to sell. It's very easy to put little links and little ads in among what people are already using from your site in order to keep your name and products in front of them all the time.

Surveys and Polls

You can do surveys and polls as a means for getting people to come to your site. Then you can spit the survey results back to them because people like to know the final results as a benchmark. You can also do live polling with this type of software...People like to come back and see current results appearing on your site as more and more respond to the poll.

Survey and polling resources:
http://www.infopoll.com
http://www.7am.com/polling/index.htm

For surveys visit:
http://www.perseus.com
http://www.zoomerang.com
http://www.surveymonkey.com
http://www.willmaster.com

Or type "survey software" or "polling software" into any search engine and you'll be given lots of different options.

E-mail Letterhead or Signature Files

One to one e-mails are sent everyday. Why not build your e-mail list while you're doing your e-mail sending each and every day. Come to Hart Creative Marketing, Inc. and start making your daily one to one e-mails work for you.

http://www.hartcreativemarketing.com/letterhead/be.html

Sales Letter (Getting Subscribers)

Search term tools
Nichebot http://www.nichebot.com
Wordtracker http://www.wordtracker.com
Overture http://www.overture.com search for suggestion tool.

Three Quarter Rule
No mention of the product until you write ¾ of the page with information. Do not make the title of the page the product name or you create sales resistance.
Headline, Subheads, Teasers, Guarantees, Scare Tactics, Urgency.

Date Script
Order by X date. Is in the code.

Domains
Place keywords in domain name

Keyword Placement
Title Bar
Top of Page
In Headline Tags
Hidden in Graphics
In Links

Keyword Density Analyzer
Inspect the amount of keyword density. Do not exceed keyword density

http://www.grsoftware.net
Or http://foreverweb.com/proshop/kda

Web Traffic Statistics (Cheap or Free)

www.visitorville.com
www.hitbox.com
www.extremetracking.com

Getting Subscribers

Make sure you have the sign up area all over your website. Provide the sign up box in every page of your site. Visit http://www.ezineuniversity.com and read its free "Handbook of Ezine Publishing." Look around and you'll see a "listing" or "announcement" sites and directories were you can list your ezine so people can find it and subscribe. This site will have the most currently list. http://www.ezineuniversity.com/courses

Biz Cards
Stationary
Voice Mail
Every Phone Call
Stickers/Labels
Promote at your programs
Advertising Specialties
Magnetic Signs
Billboards
Print ads
Product Packaging
Direct Mail
Publicity

Shopping Cart

Only the best and the most affordable for you
www.hartcreativemarketing.com

Search Engine Tips

Link Trading at Hart Creative Marketing.com (*MUST CONTROL YOUR LINKS*)

The latest study has shown that the majority of people find sites by clicking on links from other sites. Getting *LINKED* is a much more reliable way to ensure steady traffic to your site.

YOU MUST READ THIS: It has now become critically important that the actual keywords that are important to you or me are in the link text of the links that we trade. This means that if you have a link to http://www.hartcreativemarketing.com the value of it has decreased because there are no keywords in the actual link text. The links I now require for a link trade would be something like eMarketing Tips. Even though the link still points to:

http://www.hartcreativemarketing.com the link text has keywords in it that are important to me. I may have different link text that is important to me in my other sites below. You must link exactly as I tell you for us to have a deal.

You will want to think this through and decide what keywords you want in your link back from me so that your link is more valuable. It's a pretty much worthless endeavor nowadays if we don't do it this way.

Link to all of our sites listed below and we will reciprocate giving you multiple links to your site(s). This is more important than ever for search positioning because of "link popularity" -- how many links you have coming into your site from other sites *THAT HAVE THE KEYWORDS YOU WANT TO EMPHASIZE.*

Find Out Who is Linked to Your Site

http://www.linkpopularitycheck.com

Search Engine Submit Assistance

www.searchenginehelp.com   Highly Recommended
www.searchenginewatch.com

Click "Search Engine Submission Tips"

Directories

http://www.directoriezsubmission.com   Cool site that gives you a list of 200 directories where you can post your website/articles. $75 bucks.
Tip: Go to wordtracker and find out all the related terms that have to do with your product. We spent four hours and found 6100 terms that had to do with wedding receptions.

Free Horoscope Content

http://www.luckyfortune.com/webmasters.html
http://free.horoscope.com

There are many ways to have recurring information to get people to return. You don't even have to update the feeds once you put them on your site. They update themselves. Get a webmaster to find the feeds and put them on your site.

Frequent Visitor/Buyer Plans

You could start a program just like the airlines and lots of other companies. Even Radio shack has a buyer battery reward program. They give you free batteries after you buy so many.

Bookmarks

Remind people to bookmark your site so they remember to return. You can have your web designer create code that will generate a link that can easily be added to your website.

Auto-Responders

How can you automate your promotions and keep them selling for you? Many of the places that host your website give them to you for free. In other words you sign up for my Quick Tip E-newsletter you get an automatic follow up e-mail. If your hosting provider doesn't offer you auto responders....type into any search engine and affordable auto-responder services will pop right up. Hey here's an idea. I'm starting a free seven day mini course on internet marketing. When you sign up on my website, you immediately receive the first lesson and then another lesson each day for the next six days. If you'd like more information, give us a call at Hart Creative Marketing. We can help you with this wonderful marketing tool.

Or other auto-responder resources include:
http://www.hartcreativemarketing.com/hartsmart.pdf
http://www.aweber.com
http://www.getresponse.com

E-Newsletters

I always recommend the following site: http://www.e-zinez.com. If you read the entire site and follow its entire links, it will give you everything you need to know, and it will even e-mail you a template.

More resources for content:
http://www.ezinearticles.com
http://www.certificate.net
http://www.anaconda.net
http://www.website101.com/freecontent.html
http://www.ideamarketers.com
http://www.findsticky.com

Buy subscribers or send an e-mail blast:
http://www.list-builder.biz
http://innovationads.com
http://www.postmasterdirect.com
http://www.cumuli.com

How to Stuff:
http://www.e-zinez.com
http://www.ezine-tips.com
http://www.bestezines.com
http://www.ezineuniversity.com
http://www.lifestylespub.com

Other ezine directories:
http://www.ezineseek.com
http://www.webscoutlists.com
http://www.ezinesearch.com
http://www.site-city.com/members/e-zine-master
http://www.newsletteraccess.com
http://www.published.com

Getting Content

How do you get content? Ask others to write for your e-newsletter. One article site is: http://www.ezinearticles.com. You just put your articles there and other people take them or you can go there to find articles for your newsletter and all people ask is a link to their website or a link to their ezine in return. A great place to visit for articles on all kinds of topics is http://www.certificate.net.

Audio Testimonials

Make sure their not just a pat on the back. The testimonial should be customer centric, not you centric.

An example of a weak testimonial:

"Jerry, we loved your program. You were so funny. Thanks!"

Good testimonial:

"Jerry, we used your internet marketing strategies and in the first month increased our web income by 30 percent. I can't wait to implement all the other techniques you taught us."

For easy to load audio to your site, Go to:
http://members.audiogenerator.com/specialinfo.asp?x=66406

Your Own Search Engine

I'm a big fan on having your own search engine on your site so people can search your site quickly. Indirectly, this will make them want to return because they know they can find what they want quickly.

Some resources:
http://intra.whatuseek.com
http://www.searchbutton.com
http://www.searchtools.com
http://www.atomz.com
http://www.freefind.com

Viral Marketing

This can be as simple as giving out a free e-book about your topic that you allow other people to give away or sell.

Online Marketing Summary

- Discussion Boards
- Classified Ads
- Streaming News
- What's New
- Surveys and Polls
- Free Horoscope Content
- Contests and Sweepstakes
- Frequent Visitor/Buyer Plans
- E-mail Letterhead or Signature Files
- Bookmarks
- Auto-Responders
- E-Newsletters
- Your Own Search Engine
- Viral Marketing
- Getting Content
- Audio Testimonials
- Inbound Links
- Find Out Who is Linked to Your Site
- Your Own Search Engine
- Viral Marketing

Offline Marketing

Business Cards and Letterhead

All should have your website address and e-mail address.

Voice Mail

Make sure your website is mentioned on it and make sure your clear on the voice-mail. Finish every phone call if possible with, "Don't forget, go to the website and check out our free stuff. Lots of articles etc....eventually you'll have more than free stuff to give away, you'll be selling your products.

Stickers and Labels

Everything that goes out of the office should have your website address on it.

Signage

You have a magnetic sign if you have promotional vehicles.

http://www.autoplates.com
http://www.traffictalk.com

Advertising Specialties

JumpDrives customized with your logo on it! www.hotjumpdrive.com

Mouse pads, mugs, pens, monitor screen cleaners and all kinds of things can be printed with your web address listed and given away. Lots of information at: http://www.stamonline.com

Postcards and Cards

Sometimes bolstering your online campaigns with direct mail can make the difference between a great business relationship and just a prospect. There are several ways you can do cards and postcards. This is the easiest way I have found so far. This company actually addresses the envelope, stuffs the card, and adds the postage. All you have to do is chose the card, write the note, and sign it.

http://www.sendoutcards.com/11666

You can test drive this by sending an email to Bette Daoust, Ph.D. at: BetteD@BlueprintBooks.com

Offline Marketing Summary

- o Business Cards and Letterhead
- o Voice Mail
- o Stickers and Labels
- o Signage
- o Advertising Specialties
- o Postcards and Cards

NOTES

NOTES

Jerry Hart's Internet Ma$termind Mentee Program

Right now - even before you start reading my letter below - I want you to dissolve your "Comfort Zone" for the next 10 minutes.

You see, my goal here is not to change your mind about internet marketing, or anything else.

My only goal today – right here, right now - is to open your mind so that the agony of your decision making becomes so intense that your only escape is to push through your "Comfort Zone." After you're done reading this page, you can go back into your "Comfort Zone" as long as you'd like.

So if anything I've said so far is true for you, please have the willingness to read the rest of this letter. If you've read this far, the only reason you may be resisting my training is your fear that it WILL work.

I'm only guessing ... but nevertheless ... ready-or-not, here we go!

"The Most Complete Mentee Internet Program You'll Find -- *ANYWHERE*"

What is this 1 year program?
This program includes 1 year teaching you how to build a significant Internet business. You will have an exclusive VIP invitation to our 3 day Internet Mastermind Retreat Weekend as my guest. (Limited space available)

Attendance for you and guest
Spouse or Family Members included in the program can come with you for the Mastermind Retreat Weekend.

Assistants included in the program can either stay and enjoy the Bay Area or come to the training and all the activities.

The Training:
Initial Call – We schedule a talk one-on-one as initiation to breakground and get to know each other

Resource Kit – You and your guest get familiar with your kit and what it means to follow the Internet Road Map to make money on the net.

Online Training – We will take you through 30 online training sessions at your own pace. After each module you email me or call me with questions.

Teleclasses – Typically we have once-a-week conference calls – recorded if you are unable to be on the call

Reaching me for help – Unlimited phone and email assistance with me most of the time. If we find your issues surround more administrative tasks, we hope to share our wonderful staff with you to make sure any items you need addresses are handled quickly.

Critiques – This is defined as reviewing and recommending, not rewriting or redeveloping your deliverables or solutions.

Doing the work – We will illuminate pathways to success, enlighten you to strategies that really work, and critique the work YOU complete, giving you lots of recommendations.

More Details:
Referrals – We feel strongly we point you to all the resources we trust and believe will take care of you.

Visit to Internet Mastermind Retreat Weekend – Once you land in San Francisco, Oakland, your training gets underway as part of a year long program.

Free Ads – You get 2 ads in my blog

Internet Leaders eNews – Each month we highlight who's finding big wins and who may not be so we can all learn by the success and challenges of your fellow Internet Masters

Partnering for Bucks – Often times, Masters of this group will invite others into a trusted circle of biz opportunities and why not? We are watching each other make dreams come true. Sharing those dreams and working in joint venture is a fantastic way to build momentum and leverage the money and time you spent in this program.

Advanced Mastermind Groups – Many who complete this program have formed their own groups.

Analyzing and Measuring Your Ideas – My diagnosis of your direction will be straightforward and logical. I will identify and illuminate you to any strengths, weaknesses, opportunities and threats that may be in your path of internet strategies.

When do I start? – If you feel you want to wait a few months to start your Internet Mastermind Retreat Weekend. Don't worry, as we will hold a new spot for you in the following Retreat weekend, held several times throughout the year.

Free Teleseminars – When I open my teleseminars or webcast to the public you are invited in to participate for FREE or you may request a recording.

My Cell Phone Number – This success you achieve is so important to me you will be able to reach me on my cel phone.

Copywriting or Content – If you see any ad copy of mine you want to steal, I'm more than happy to share.

No Risk Guarantee:
This is a non-refundable. However, if after one full year you don't have a profitable Internet business then by all means, your money is returned. It's not in my best interest
to not refund when you have called or emailed your progress report every two weeks minimum, completed your assignments, and have consistently worked to build your internet business. I would never accept anyone person bad mouthing my intent to truly help people start, grow and maintain a million dollar internet business. Thanks for your integrity and support in advance.

Visit us at www.hartcreativemarketing.com to find out more!

FAX TO 925.281.0228
Email us at info@hartcreativemarketing.com

"How Can We Help You Today?"

Regards,

Jerry Hart
CEO
Hart Creative Marketing, Inc.
www.hartcreativemarketing.com

Index

NOTES

eMarketing
The Seminar

This seminar is part of the Blueprints for Success series of books for business. The impetus behind the series was to provide exactly what I wished had been available when I started my first business. These books are meant to be a guide for those who are not quite sure of how to start. And for those veterans in the business world, this book offers a new perspective on old procedures and new ones. In a nutshell, it is the business world through my eyes and how these methods worked for me. I have taught these methods to many people and to my children who have told me numerous times that they appreciated how I view the world of business and taught them to do the same. This book may not be for everyone but I think that everyone should have one. The methods and tips in this book are a valuable part of business and should be part of your business library.

Title in the Blueprints for Success series include:

Blueprints for Success - Networking
Blueprints for Success - Leadership
Blueprints for Success - Branding Yourself

Other titles:

The Credit Repair Kit
Marketing Magic!

Future titles:

Blueprints for Success - Discovery Selling
Blueprints for Success - Workforce Mobility
Blueprints for Success - Publicity
Blueprints for Success - Marketing

Interested in being one of our authors? Send an email with your proposal to author@blueprintbooks.com

Be sure to look for additional titles on our website:
www.BlueprintBooks.com

Quick Order Form

Blueprint Books
Blueprints for Success

Fax Orders: 800-605-2914

Telephone Orders: Call 800-605-2913 toll free.
Have your credit card ready.

Email Orders:
orders@BlueprintBooks.com

Postal Orders:
Blueprint Books
PO Box 10757,
Pleasanton, CA 94588 USA

Please send the following books, discs or reports. I understand that I may return any of them for a full refund-for any reason, no questions asked.

_____

Please send more FREE information on:

[ ] Other books [ ] Speaking/Seminars [ ] Consulting

Name: _____
Address: _____
        City: _____ State: _____ Zip: _____
Telephone: _____
Email address: _____

Sales tax: Please add 8.75% for products shipped to California addresses.
Shipping by Air: US $5.00 for the first book and $3.00 for each additional product.
International: $10 for first book or disk; $6.00 for each additional product (estimate).

Payment: [ ] Check [ ] Credit Card:
        [ ] Visa [ ] MasterCard [ ] American Express

Card Number: _____

Name on card: _____
Expiration Date: ____/_____ (month/year)